DON'T STOP BELIEVIN'

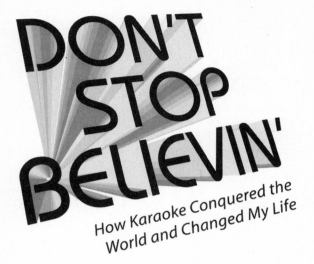

DON'T STOP BELIEVIN'

How Karaoke Conquered the
World and Changed My Life

BY BRIAN RAFTERY

Chloe —
I look forward to
Theo's first karaoke party!
Brian R

Da Capo Press
A Member of the Perseus Books Group

Designed by Timm Bryson

Set in 10.5 point Warnock by The Perseus Books Group

Library of Congress Cataloging-in-Publication Data
Raftery, Brian.
    Don't stop believin': how karaoke conquered the world
and changed my life / by Brian Raftery.
        p. cm.
    ISBN 978-0-306-81583-6 (alk. paper)
    1. Karaoke—Social aspects. 2. Karaoke—History and
criticism. 3. Raftery, Brian. I. Title.
  ML3918.K36R35 2008
  782.42164—dc22

                                2008034271

Published by Da Capo Press
A Member of the Perseus Books Group
www.dacapopress.com

Da Capo Press books are available at special discounts for
bulk purchases in the U.S. by corporations, institutions,
and other organizations. For more information, please
contact the Special Markets Department at the Perseus
Books Group, 2300 Chestnut Street, Suite 200,
Philadelphia, PA 19103, or call (800) 810-4145, ext. 5000,
or e-mail special.markets@perseusbooks.com.

10 9 8 7 6 5 4 3 2 1

To my Nana Mac,
who always hated Mel Tormé

Here people could sing unrestrained; and sing they did with heart and gusto, under all circumstances and on all conceivable subjects: noble and inspiring, playful and humorous, sentimental and nostalgic, boisterous and zestful. Farmers, city dwellers, soldiers, sailors, cowboys, lumberjacks, slaves, prisoners—rich and poor, young and old—they all sang, from the Atlantic to the Pacific, from Bunker Hill to Broadway.

—DENES AGAY, *Best Loved Songs of the American People*, 1975

I felt very like a duck out of water.

—FORMER U.S. ATTORNEY GENERAL JANET RENO, DESCRIBING HER FIRST AND ONLY KARAOKE EXPERIENCE TO *The New Yorker*, OCTOBER 2007

CONTENTS

Nomihoodai

I T'S OKAY WITH ME IF YOU HATE KARAOKE. BUT ASK YOURSELF: DO YOU *REALLY* WANT TO BE LIKE DON HENLEY?

Henley, one of the cofounders of the Eagles, is famous for being a sanctimonious knob, a guy who takes his music—which ranges from arid to somewhat arid—quite seriously. He's always been a go-to target for music critics, many of whom don't believe his discography warrants his arrogance, and in 1990, he even inspired a song called "Don Henley Must Die," in which rockabilly singer Mojo Nixon called for his demise. I was always split on Henley: While I couldn't forgive his innate smugness, I did love "All She Wants to Do Is Dance," one of the more jaunty songs ever written about U.S. foreign policy. Then I found out he doesn't want people to sing his songs at karaoke.

In fact, Henley actually forbids karaoke companies from rerecording songs in his catalog, whether they're from his solo career or from his time with the Eagles. These karaoke recordings still exist, of course, but they're often black-market bootlegs, meaning that anyone who's ever gotten a bit zonked and performed "The

Boys of Summer" or "Hotel California" at a bar may have been un-knowingly propping up an obscure and niche-specific criminal enterprise. Henley's not the only artist to impose such sanctions, and yet he seems to incite the most animosity among karaoke-industry professionals: A few years ago, a karaoke-music company called Sound Choice put out a compilation entitled *Hits of the Don & Friends, Vol. 1*, an inside-joke fuck-you that included a num-ber of songs Henley had performed, but not written, and there-fore couldn't forbid from being turned into karaoke tracks (when it comes to diss albums, the karaoke industry tends to be very passive-aggressive). And while Sound Choice has more than 17,000 rerecordings in its catalog, it only carries a single Mojo Nixon song. You can probably guess which one.

I can't fathom why a performer like Henley would be so stingy with his songs, denying his fans the opportunity to perform them. Having your music retrofitted for karaoke is a high honor, and val-idation that people will always love your songs, even if you're not the one performing them. Clearly, Henley's famous '80s-era pony-tail was merely the mop head on a stick lodged far up his butt.

But maybe I'm taking this a tad too personally.

After all, I *love* karaoke. I love it without qualifiers, apologies, or actual singing talent. When people talk about the adrenaline rush that comes with playing competitive sports or putting angel dust on their eyelids, I think, "Yes, fine, but have you ever performed 'Bennie and the Jets' in a hot tub?" For years, I've employed karaoke as both a stimulant and an antidepressant, and I've trav-eled the world seeking out the perfect karaoke experience, whether it's in a Filipino bar in Vienna or a wedding reception in South Dakota. My affection for karaoke is so severe, I've even made two separate trips to Japan, the place where the words *kara* (empty) and *okestura* (orchestra) were first combined, and where the art of the sing-along has undergone nearly forty years of scrutiny and refinement. In Japan, you can sing all over the city, from minuscule private rooms (called "k-boxes," for karaoke box) to lavishly futuristic suites. The Japanese even have a special karaoke password: *nomihoodai.* It's pronounced like a Scottish pimp's lament—*no, me ho die*—and it somehow translates as "unlimited drink." When used properly, *nomihoodai* will yield nonstop trays of cheap beers, which will invariably be delivered by a cute waitress. Going to Japan for karaoke isn't so much a vacation as it is a pilgrimage, a heaven on earth where you can actually perform Belinda Carlisle's "Heaven Is a Place on Earth."

I always suspected there were other karaoke fiends out there, but up until a few years ago, I couldn't find many of them. From 1999 to 2002, when my friends and I were going to New York City karaoke bars on just about every other weekend, I'd often invite coworkers or casual acquaintances to come along with us, and they usually looked at me as though I'd just asked them to help officiate a cockfight. In many ways, I empathized with their reluctance, as I've suffered for my karaoke pursuits. You don't know the human body's threshold for pain until you've been stuck on a Scandinavian cruise ship at two in the morning, watching an international karaoke contest and listening to "My Heart Will Go On" for the third time in as many hours; it's enough to make you consider those rolling black sheets of the Baltic Sea as a viable exit strategy. Karaoke requires the willingness to be entertained by strangers, and many of those strangers are complete chuckleheads, including myself. So I understand why some people still dismiss it as a lowbrow lark and are repulsed by the idea of going anywhere near a karaoke bar. I've simply learned to treat these people the same way my religious friends treat me: outwardly supportive, but always secretly hoping for an awakening.

Over time, I've attempted some of these conversions myself, recruiting skeptics to join me and my friends at our belovedly dinky karaoke bar in New York City's East Village. So long as these novices can withstand the sober, inevitably uneasy first thirty minutes, they usually end up realizing that karaoke is a way to broadcast those songs that have been playing in their heads for years. At a time when songs and albums are widely distributed but often privately indulged, karaoke is simply a communal form of music appreciation.

This may be why, after twenty years of being perpetually derided by Americans, karaoke has finally become an accepted part of our culture—so much so that it's rarely employed as an easy punchline. In the time that I worked on this book, karaoke was featured on *The Sopranos, Ugly Betty,* and *The Office;* endorsed publicly by Norah Jones, Nick Cave, and French president Nicolas Sarkozy; and referenced at least twice in the comic strip *Garfield.* There were even two competing prime-time karaoke-related television shows, *The Singing Bee* and *Don't Forget the Lyrics,* both of which debuted on the same week. And with the exception of Garfield (who's still haughtily commenting on the ever-pressing social matters of 1986), not one of these entities mocked karaoke. Rather, it was invoked as a normal part of day-to-day life, one that transcended all obstructions of class, race, or ethnicity. No program more deftly encapsulated karaoke's newfound outreach than the football drama *Friday Night Lights,* which found its characters singing not only in a Mexican brothel, but also in a small-town Texas megachurch, where parishioners sang along with lyrics printed on giant TV screens.

I first noticed this cultural reversal a few years ago, when the reliably desolate k-box bars that my friends and I had been frequenting on the Lower East Side suddenly became jammed with singers. These were places that you could once walk into on a moment's notice and easily get a room; now they had hours-long waiting lists. What happened?

For starters, unlike such faddish imports as Tamagotchi or socialism, karaoke refused to go away, even in the face of widespread apathy. The first karaoke machines were invented by the Japanese in 1971, and though they looked a bit like an 8-track machine mating with a CB radio, it didn't take long for the devices to spread through Asia. But when the first karaoke machines arrived stateside in the early '80s, many Americans refused to even go near them, for fear of looking stupid in front of their peers. Yet a handful of determined entrepreneurs kept pushing karaoke around the country, slowly building a loyal audience of aspiring singers and homesick foreigners. By the turn of the century, an entire generation had come of age without the same performance-anxiety issues that plagued their forebears, and karaoke had become a multimillion-dollar industry.

And during that maddeningly slow twenty-year ascent, the traditional relationship between performer and audience had been dramatically redefined. From the very beginning of time—when the first protozoan life-form crawled atop a rock and sang "Love Shack" to a horny newt—there's been an accepted division between those who have demonstrable musical talent and those who do not. That barrier still exists today, but it's easier to vault—or at least it's perceived as being easier. *American Idol* and the popular video game *Guitar Hero* have sold the idea that musical talent is no longer the exclusive domain of professionals but something that's available to all. Fans used to see musicians on stage and think, "How did they do that?" Now they watch and wonder, "When do *I* get to do that?" To teenagers and early twentysomethings growing up in our increasingly emulative culture, a karaoke bar isn't just a hangout. It's a rehearsal space.

I took very few notes during my peak years of karaoke abuse, and as a result, most of my recollections of that time run together in one long, unmelodious montage. I don't remember what I sang at that Filipino bar in Austria, but I do know that I was one of the few people *not* to choose a Lionel Richie's "Hello." Nor do I recall the name of my bartender in Barcelona, who sang Lou Rawls's "You're Going to Miss My Loving" as an anti-U.S. rally roared on only a few blocks away. And I certainly don't know when (or why) my friends and I began our tradition of huddling together to sing Boyz II Men songs, even if we weren't actually anywhere near a karaoke bar. This last bit has been going on for nearly ten years now, even though the joke is funny to exactly five people. It's hard to say goodbye to yesterday when you insist upon still living in it.

As ridiculous as it might sound, though, nights like these forever changed my life. Karaoke bars are where I've fallen in and out of love, struggled with friendships, and generally observed the world at large. Much of my twenties and early thirties were accompanied by the sound of cheaply produced, vaguely familiar instrumental backing tracks, and even today, it often seems as though the only way I can truly connect with others is through song—even if I do sometimes struggle to remember the right words. But in the past three years, my karaoke excursions have become less frequent. Private-room karaoke in Manhattan isn't cheap—with alcohol, even a small group can wind up with a $200-plus tab—and I recently developed asthma, which causes me to gasp for breath after only two songs; my biggest fear is that I'll asphyxiate halfway through "The Humpty Dance" and then get stuck with a posthumous $50 room-rental charge. An even greater karaoke impediment is age: Now that all of my friends are into their thirties, there are greater responsibilities to consider, and spending three hours in a karaoke room is difficult to justify when you've got an early-morning commute or a shrieking newborn at home.

As it became clear that my karaoke heyday was winding down, I decided to spend a year investigating my own obsession, traveling around the country and the world to meet fellow karaoke enthusiasts. There were spastic metalheads in New York, costumed seniors in Hawaii, and more drunken Europeans in Bangkok than I could possibly count (or keep up with). I got to meet some of the people who'd inadvertently launched all of these singing careers, like Daisuke Inoue, the Japanese inventor credited with building the first karaoke machine, and the employees at Sound Choice, the North Carolina company whose backing tracks I'd been singing along with for years. And, of course, I visited every karaoke bar I could, singing with friends old and new. It was the loudest year of my life, and throughout it all, I couldn't stop thinking about Don Henley.

Again, I don't have anything personal against the Don; it's just that, in my view, he's become the smirking emissary for all those who deride karaoke without experiencing it. Whenever I walked into a new karaoke bar, I'd often imagine what it would be like to grab Henley by the bolo tie and drag him in against his will, just so he could watch these novice singers temporarily recast themselves as stars. He'd see the joy that comes with uncorking these songs from their bodies. He'd learn that, in moments of boozy clarity, Billy Joel's "Scenes from an Italian Restaurant" sounds like a really good rap song, while Naughty by Nature's "Everything's Gonna Be Alright" sounds like a really bad Billy Joel song. Maybe he'd ask why people do this every night, and after I told him about all the karaoke adventures I'd had around the world, he'd want to sign up for a song.

"So how does this all work, exactly?" Don Henley would ask. "You just get up there and start singing along with the TV?"

"Oh, Don Henley," I'd sigh, opening the songbook and turning on the microphone. "Maybe I should go first."

CHAPTER 1

Village People

I WAS TEN YEARS OLD WHEN I REALIZED I COULDN'T SING. AT THE OUTER BOUNDARIES OF MY ELEMENTARY SCHOOL PLAYGROUND—AS FAR away from the athletic equipment as possible—sat a row of chain-link swingsets that doubled as my own private outdoor amphitheater. Every time we broke for recess, I'd plop down on the thick rubber seat, kick the dirt for momentum, and serenade my unsuspecting classmates in a screech.

"Her name is Ree-yo," I'd yelp, pumping my legs harder and higher with each verse, "And she dances in the saaaaand . . ."

This was in the mid-'80s, long before commercial-radio playlists became timid and fractured, and on most weekday nights, I'd hide my FM Walkman under the pillow, kept awake by the sounds of rap, rock, and post-disco, all of them aligning on the same frequency. The next afternoon, I'd recite as many songs as I could remember, even if I couldn't remember them correctly: Duran Duran, the Beastie Boys, Wham!, Michael Jackson, Run-D.M.C., and "Weird Al" Yankovic. I did my best to whisper the more provocative lyrics, but most double entendres were well beyond my fourth-grade education. Years later, when I finally de-ciphered Cyndi Lauper's "She Bop," I realized I'd spent a good por-tion of my recess time screaming about vibrators.

At the end of each performance, just as I was about to spring into orbit, I'd drag my sneakers into the ground and look at the seats next to mine. Usually, they were empty. I can't blame my classmates for distancing themselves from me, as my prepubes-cent voice made an awful racket, one that's almost impossible to put across in print. The only way to re-create that sound today would be to (1) obtain a magical talking seagull; (2) lock that sea-gull in a room for three months with little nourishment and a copy of *Thriller* on a loop; (3) record whatever noise came out of its mouth when you opened the door.

Still, I kept singing whenever I could, whether it was at Sunday school or Little League games. At the time, I didn't think it was unusual for a kid to go around barking out lyrics; I was just bored and spazzy, and constantly searching for new songs to memorize. So I scrutinized every entry in the Top 40, and when I was finished with them, I read old *Rolling Stone* magazine album guides and tried to guess what certain songs must have sounded like, based on their titles alone. I'd then record these songs a cappella style into a portable cassette recorder, along with a few of my own composi-tions, including 1985's indelible "Who's Afraid of the Dark?" which went like this:

> *Who's afraid?*
> *Who's afraid?*
> *Who's afraid of the dark?*

Simplistic, yes, but still on par with just about anything ever written by Tom Waits.

In the fall of 1988, my family moved from the suburbs of Philadelphia to the suburbs of Honolulu. My father had been working as a foreign news editor at the *Philadelphia Inquirer*, and when he received an Asian studies grant at the University of Hawaii, we relocated to a suburban home with a view of the mountains and a poorly scrambled Playboy Channel. This should have been the most amazing time of my life, but I was just about to begin seventh grade, which had long been promised as the darker, edgier sequel to sixth grade—a year in which everyone back in my school in Pennsylvania would allegedly get to drink, feel each other up, and go to colonial Williamsburg. I would likely have been socially ineligible for two-thirds of these activities, yet I still felt cheated, and spent most of my ten months in Honolulu sulking around a comic-book store and listening to Tracy Chapman and *Appetite for Destruction*. While in Hawaii, though, I did pick up two important new vocabulary words. The first was *haole* (how-lee), a slightly derogatory Hawaiian word for "white person." The second was *karaoke*.

My father's Asian studies curriculum included a survey on Japanese culture, and because Hawaii's population at that time was nearly 25 percent Japanese, this allowed for occasional in-the-field observations. One night, he and several of his mostly *haole* classmates wound up at a karaoke bar in a downtown Honolulu strip mall, where they watched the Japanese and Korean patrons carry on their century-old tradition of mutual animosity (apparently, the Japanese host was haranguing some of the Koreans for being lousy tippers, which seems like a counterintuitive way to obtain further tips). It was into this marginally hostile environment that my father, a bit soused, got up and sang Frank Sinatra's "New York, New York." When my mother informed me of this the next day, I was mystified: Though he loved music, my father sang even less than he drank—which was just about never—and he'd never once hinted at a desire to perform. In fact, he'd always seemed ashamed of his voice, so much so that when he sang in church, he did it at the lowest possible volume, trying to avoid judgment from anyone who was listening, higher power or otherwise. Yet at this karaoke bar, in full view of his classmates and the greater public, he'd made it through not just a few refrains, but an entire song. To this day, whenever I try to imagine what it must have been like to watch him sing in that bar, there's a dotted, empty outline in the middle. I can build the interior and fill in the seats, but I can never actually *see* him.

We returned to Pennsylvania in 1989, and any time I wanted to deflect my classmates' questions about my lack of a tan—an unforeseen result of that sporadic Playboy Channel access—I'd quickly change the subject to my father's karaoke excursion. This was mostly greeted with incredulous looks, even though everyone in my town had long ago learned to accept the Mummers Parade, an annual Philadelphia pageant in which teamsters play banjos and wear bird outfits. Somehow, this homoerotic *Island of Dr. Moreau* went unquestioned, while karaoke struck my classmates as flamboyant and strange. Unfortunately, there was no way to convince them otherwise, because none of us were actually old enough to experience a karaoke bar for ourselves. It existed entirely in the abstract, which is probably why it was so easy to make fun of in the first place.

I soon forgot about karaoke and carried forth with my burgeoning musical career, joining a junior-high choral group and taking guitar lessons. Both were just fronts for my master plan, which was to form a cover band as a backing guitarist, and then eventually wrestle power from the lead singer in a bloodless but still theatrical coup. Cover bands were everywhere in my school, mostly because nothing in the suburbs could ever be so dramatic as to inspire you to actually write your *own* songs. Instead, most bands chose from an unofficial list of about thirty or so classic-rock numbers, leading to asinine debates over who "owned" certain songs. If anything sums up how relatively stress-free it was to be in high school in the early '90s—just a few years before mandatory metal detectors and see-through backpacks became commonplace—it's the fact that my biggest adolescent fear was that some other band might learn the Who's "Baba O'Riley" before we could.

Our band had a suitably unoriginal name—Crosstown Traffic—and I only played a few "gigs," mostly at teen-center events and school talent programs. I recently watched a fifteen-year-old tape of our performance, and I cannot possibly appear more uncomfortable on stage: As the band plays Creedence Clearwater Revival's "Fortunate Son," I'm hunching over my guitar in the corner, failing at the only thing I really cared about. I quit Crosstown Traffic a few months later.

Despite these setbacks, I kept singing, even if it was just to myself. Not in an unhinged-loony kind of way, mind you—I'm not the old guy standing behind you at the convenience store, screaming "Can-Can" way too loud, though that is my inevitable fate. But every day, some song bribes its way into my head and loiters there for hours, and the only way to kick it out is to sing it; like a cry of pain or a laughing fit, it's a reflexive, uncontrollable act. I see the similarly afflicted everywhere I go: at the gym, where the weightlifters grunt along to some terrible Creed anthem without realizing it, or on the subway, where commuters shut their eyes and move their lips, forgetting they're being watched by others.

I've even seen it at my local bagel shop, where—after more than a year of nothing but frowning transactions—the woman behind the counter one day broke character and started singing along with a Trisha Yearwood ballad on the radio. Remarkably, she managed to keep on scowling while she did this. But for a moment, her instincts got the better of her.

To sing aloud is a natural urge, as just about every important moment of our lives is marked with song. We're treated to lullabies on our first days and hymns on our last—though we never quite get a chance to appreciate them—and in between, there are birthday parties, church gatherings, road trips, weddings, and camping trips, all of which require us to raise our voices, even if we do so reluctantly. Underneath all the social barriers like headphones and iPods, we're just a world of singing fools. If we were to drop all the niceties and just happily let rip with whatever tunes were in our heads, the streets would be filled with people hooting and hollering nonstop, as it was hundreds of years ago:

1290 B.C. (est.)—Every third event in the Old Testament is marked with women singing: the parting of the Red Sea, David killing the Philistines, etc. If the Bible is even partially accurate, being around the Israelites was like being at a Luther Vandross concert.

Tenth century—Gregorians be chantin'.

1620—Passengers on the *Mayflower* head off to the New World carrying small books of psalms.

Mid-1700s—Slaves are brought over to America, using songs to pray and teach.

1770s—Newspaper articles begin running "Broadside Ballads," which are essentially op-eds and articles presented in sing-along form.

1835—*The Southern Harmony and Musical Companion,* one of the first widely distributed songbooks, is released.

1843—The first minstrel show, *We're All Going to Regret This Someday,* opens in New York.

1860s—Home piano sales rise in America.

1861–1865—Armies from the North and South pledge their allegiances using Civil War songs.

1870s—The Fisk Jubilee Singers, a gospel vocal group, become one of the first superstar acts to sing around the world.

1870s—Singing cowboys somehow avoid getting beaten up.

1890s—Tin Pan Alley sheet music takes off, thanks in part to "song pushers," who are hired by publishers to go into a community and get them to sing.

1901—Pedal-operated Pianolas—which use paper rolls to reproduce popular hits of the day—drop in price, gaining them newfound popularity.

1924—The first sing-along cartoon, *Ko-Ko Song Car-Tune,* debuts in New York City, imploring audience members to "follow the bouncing ball." Two decades later, the same bouncing-ball format would be used for World War II shorts.

1961—*Sing Along with Mitch,* a prime-time musical revue starring Mitch Miller—who looks a bit like Vincent Price, but more menacing, if that's even possible—premieres on NBC.

For centuries, singing was a communal undertaking, one that could serve as a religious lesson, a narrative, or simply a way to tally one's bananas. It didn't hurt if you were talented at it, of course, but I'm guessing that if the cowboys were singing, everybody else was, too.

By the time I was born, though, it had long been established that singing was an act best left to *real* singers, even the annoying ones, like theater majors. When prerecorded music became popular after the end of World War I, our relationship with music became far less collaborative. The songs that had been handed down through generations were no longer in danger of suddenly becoming extinct; they could be now recorded for posterity. And whereas sheet music and Pianolas demanded a certain amount of interactivity from music lovers, the phonograph allowed listeners to simply buy a professionally recorded version of their favorite song and play it nonstop, without having to worry about learning the song themselves.

Most importantly, the advent of prerecorded music soon gave rise to pop stars, and I think this is when people *really* started to become more self-conscious about their voices. Our ancestors didn't have to worry about what their voices sounded like—they just *sang*, because they could. Who cared whether or not they had talent? They just needed something to do while fermenting rotgut liquor. But the popular-performer era established a hierarchy of vocal talent, and suddenly, there was an accepted criteria for what constituted "good" and "bad" singing. In the early 1920s, you might have had the best voice in your church choir, but once people heard Bessie Smith's version of "Downhearted Blues," yours was just above average. Bessie Smith knocked you on your ass, and everybody knew it.

By 1986, the year I started singing in that playground, most people were familiar with how a song like "Rio" was supposed to sound, including myself. I didn't need critics or teachers or fleeing classmates to tell me that I had a lousy voice; all I had to do was listen to the radio. This might explain why I was so embarrassed whenever my mom would walk around our house singing Johnny

Mathis holiday songs and various Broadway showtunes. It wasn't that her singing was bad—it was just that she wasn't as good as the "proper" recorded version. She wasn't *supposed* to be singing.

So I lived quietly, keeping my songs to myself, and only allowing them out at recess, by which time they were so pent up that I couldn't hold back any longer. And then, more than ten years later, I discovered karaoke, and I haven't been able to shut up ever since.

As was the case with so many other ludicrous pursuits I picked up in my twenties—malt liquor, ska, polyester suits—I was finally talked into karaoke by my friend Mike.

I met Mike in the fall of 1994 at Penn State University, where we'd later become roommates. I couldn't understand why he'd want to hang out with me: He had a girlfriend and sideburns, two by-products of a confidence I couldn't possibly have possessed at that age. But he was as bored as I was in central Pennsylvania, and thus spent the next four years developing as many hobbies as he could, often abandoning them within months, if not weekends. In the time I've known him, his list of on-again, off-again fixations has grown to include Krav Maga, DJing, shoplifting meat, *Quake,* reggaeton, feeding stray geese, call-in talk-radio shows, tattoos, break-dancing lessons, flaxseed oil pills, PlayStations 1 through 3, motorcycling, motor-scootering, skeet-shooting, creatine supplements, Capoeira, and possible enrollment in the Guardian Angels.

Mike owned a car, so on weekends we'd grab a wallet of CDs and go for long drives to the small towns outside of school, even though there was nothing to do when we got there, except to poke around depressing thrift shops and eat fast food. These trips were mostly an excuse to sing along to the radio, which we did for hours; somehow, I'd met the only other person in the world who didn't think it was weird to let loose with whatever song was currently partying in his head. We'd both grown up in the suburbs, which meant that our shared musical tastes consisted of our mothers' '70s AM-gold collections, classic rock, and modern hip-hop, and we'd drive around Route 80, alternating between Carly Simon and the Wu-Tang Clan. We didn't have sports or fraternity events to bond over, and the video games back then weren't that good. So we sat in a car and tried to remember the right words to "You're So Vain" and "Shame on a Nigga" while eating McFlurries.

Mike had first discovered karaoke after using a borrowed I.D. to sneak into a bar on Long Island. He was nineteen at the time and made a mistake common to so many first-time karaoke singers: He chose "Free Bird." Mike was only tangentially familiar with the song and therefore didn't realize that "Free Bird" went on for nearly nine minutes, during which the vocal parts pretty much excuse themselves and wander around the parking lot. This leaves the singer without a whole lot to do, aside from desperately air-guitaring or maybe making a few errant hoots. Mike flailed his way through the song's finale, and when it was over, he was wounded, but also enlightened. At that point in his life, Mike was most interested in singing, drinking, and behaving clownishly in public, but until karaoke, he'd had to pursue all those interests separately. "Karaoke was the union," he told me several years later. "These three things, put together."

He spent his next few years at Penn State trying to find a local karaoke venue, often with discouraging results, as karaoke in our region was scarce. His most notable success came on a Saturday afternoon in the spring of 1997, when he and our mutual friend

Kevin discovered a temporary karaoke jockey, or "KJ," who'd set up a stage in the middle of our local mall. At the time, Garth Brooks was in the middle of a local five-night concert run, so the KJ had only thought to bring along country songs and rock ballads. It was a limited song selection, yet even then, Mike could divine the absurd. Whenever he scanned a weak karaoke book, he could always find that one weirdly anachronistic song that the rest of us had overlooked. It was as though the soundtrack for that *exact* moment stood out from all those lines of text and announced itself to him.

Mike and Kevin turned in their song choice, and after the KJ got a look at their selection and their reformed-skateboarder attire, he immediately put them in the back of the queue. A half-hour passed, and as soon as one of the shoppers finished his rousing version of Neil Diamond's "America"—a performance that prompted swells of patriotic applause—Mike and Kevin took to the stage and began singing Tag Team's "Whoomp! (There It Is)." Not long into the song, Kevin began jumping up and down, elbowing Mike in the jaw; by the time they got to the *boom-shock-a-locka* parts, the audience members' reactions had shifted from confusion to revulsion. These people did not enjoy being whoomped against their will.

"You never realize how long that song actually is," Mike says now, "until you do it in front of a crowd that hates every second of it."

I wish I'd accompanied Mike on this trip, as well as the other karaoke expeditions he took between 1997 and 1998. But the very idea of getting up in front of others, much less *singing* to them, terrified me. My brief high-school rock-band career had provided enough residual shame to last a lifetime, and after four years of eating cereal out of a family-serving salad bowl, I'd become recklessly overweight (not quite obese, perhaps, but definitely post-husky). I was far too self-conscious for something as vulnerable as karaoke.

A few months before Mike was to graduate and move to Manhattan, a weekly karaoke night opened up at a sports bar just a few blocks off campus. Mike insisted I go with him, noting that the place was all but abandoned, and that if we went with a group of friends, it would be like our own private karaoke party. I relented, mostly because I'd run out of things to do at night in Central Pennsylvania, and because I could always back out at the last minute. By then, I'd worked out a reliable awkwardness-avoidance strategy: Show up someplace new, indicate some sort of vague illness by rubbing my belly and squinting, and then depart using whatever alternative travel arrangements I'd planned out beforehand. This bar would be especially easy to escape, because it was within walking distance of our house, and because it was one of the least popular bars near campus. When we walked in, I immediately understood why: It smelled like Sam Adams. Not the beer, mind you, but the actual New England revolutionary, indignant and pee-ridden under the floorboards.

We took to the back of the bar with a beer pitcher and the songbook. The place wasn't quite as deserted as I'd hoped, but the few customers scattered about didn't even seem to notice that we were there. Maybe I *could* do this, I thought. Karaoke didn't seem too different from singing with my friends in the car. Besides, Mike had been cajoling me to try karaoke for months, and he was usually right about such things: During our junior year, for example, he'd convinced me to spend the last $25 in my bank account on a full-body California Raisin costume, one that had no doubt been made by hand in 1983. As I walked around town that night, laughing at myself under my costume, I decided that I could probably stand to take a few more risks in my life, even if those risks involved me dressing up like a giant raisin. After all, Mike didn't care what anyone else thought about him, and it seemed like an incredibly liberating way to live.

So I agreed to try karaoke, with the stipulation that we signed up as a group—that way, we could trade off verses, in case I got uneasy. There were still a few other volunteers ahead of us, and their performances gave me enough time to regret my decision. I began formulating elaborate excuses as to why I could not, under any circumstances, sing at this bar: *I don't remember how the chorus goes. My throat feels a little itchy.* I was about to come down with one of my trademark bouts of hallucinatory nausea when our group's name was called.

We walked from the back of the bar to the karaoke rig, which was a small portable monitor on a stand; I hid in the back of our group, obscuring myself from view. As for the performance itself, there are conflicting accounts as to what song we chose: I seem to recall the words to Stevie Wonder's "Signed, Sealed, Delivered I'm Yours" appearing in front of me, though no one else can verify that. What I do remember is that, at some point during the song, I began to feel calm, as though all the tension in my body—tension that had been collecting for twenty years—was suddenly vanquished. As far as I was concerned, there was no audience; just me, my friends, and this song, whatever song it might have been.

After our turn was over, there was applause and some slippery high fives, and I returned to our table, where I'd remain for the rest of the night: I knew the sudden fit of joy I'd just experienced could quickly be negated if I got greedy. As I watched my friends return to the front of the bar for an unsolicited encore of Aqua's "Barbie Girl," I sat in the back, trying to figure out what had just happened. Only a few minutes ago, I'd been calculating every possible way in which I could embarrass myself, and none of them had come true.

I'd spent the last few years being terrified of karaoke. What else had I been wrong about?

Within about ten minutes of moving from Penn State to New York City—or more specifically, to the suburbs of New Jersey, where I was living while interning at *Entertainment Weekly* magazine— Mike brought me down to a two-floor private-room karaoke bar he'd discovered not long after arriving in Manhattan. With two long hallways branching into sixteen smaller rooms, Village Karaoke looked like a walk-in health clinic, and at times, it felt like one: The check-in process was long and confusing, the bills were loaded with unforeseen costs, and at least one person in the waiting room always looked to be near death.

Mike had become enthralled with private rooms, or k-boxes, during a five-month stay in Osaka. Because he was accustomed to public karaoke available back home, he was initially disappointed when he realized that the biggest k-box audience in Japan would be no larger than twelve overly snug-fitting attendees. But after a long inaugural evening of *nomihoodai,* he realized that in a private room, he could sing for hours on end, without having to wait for a bunch of other people to get their turn. Even the performances became more collaborative, as people could pick up a microphone and join in whenever they wanted. After my first night singing at Village, I felt even more at ease than I had at that Pennsylvania sports bar, as there were no unknown onlookers. I knew maybe five people in the city, and I could fit them all, just barely, in the cheapest room.

Village Karaoke became our by-the-hour social club, a place where we could drop in whenever we wanted, and where no one would ever tell us to turn down the music. At first, we'd only visit once or twice a month. By the fall of 1999, almost every weekend seemed to end with a cab ride there, and "Bowery between Fifth and Sixth" became the first New York City address I knew by heart. Some nights, I didn't even know why our small group of friends even bothered to go anywhere else, because within half an hour of walking into some party or bar, all we wanted to do was to go to Village Karaoke.

Part of the allure was Village Karaoke's songbook, which included thousands of Top 40 songs from the late '60s to the late '90s, plus lots of random material that was simply filed under "Standard" or "Various." On any given night, one could have walked by our room and heard Shaggy's "Boombastic" followed by Petula Clark's "Downtown" followed by "Hava Nagila." We used a remote control to enter track numbers, but because much of the library was stored within a giant bank of laser-discs, songs often took forever to load, and sometimes disappeared altogether. I imagined they were being sucked into an alternate-realm vortex, where some poor soul was being subjected to "Love Is a Battle-field" three times a night.

We invited everyone we knew to Village Karaoke, no matter what kind of music they liked. There were metalheads, fashion executives, and French people, and one of our parties was crashed by a group of Japanese punk-rockers dressed as samurais. The sessions would go until two or three in the morning, often because we had nowhere else to go. We couldn't afford to get into nightclubs and parties, and even if we could, we surely would have been shooed away by the dot-commers who were then running the city. As absurd as it was, this was our own downtown-Manhattan music scene, even though any *real* musicians who happened to walk into our room would surely have turned around and fled. Everyone who moves to New York City does so to make a claim on it, no matter how small; if you can walk past just one corner and feel a sense of ownership—if you can say, "That was mine," even though you never actually paid the rent—then you've succeeded. At Village Karaoke, we managed to create something new, in a city where every idea and cultural movement had been wrung out a million times before.

Mike was the de facto host for these karaoke nights, and he developed some very specific rules. These were never actually spelled out, and they were rarely enforced, yet we still live by many of them today:

- No "flippers," that is, people who have no intention of singing, yet spend hours flipping through the songbooks, pretending to look for the right track. At Village Karaoke, both the songbooks and our capacity were extremely limited, and thus flippers were politely given the gas-face until they either surrendered the book or left altogether.

- If you picked a song and then just stood there as it played, all the while making a confused, apologetic expression, the other people in the room were legally entitled to hit the "cancel" button within one minute. The queue was almost always an hour deep, and it had to be constantly pruned and maintained so that everyone would get to sing (by that same measure, if you accidentally canceled someone else's song in mid-performance, you had to reenter it immediately).

- The following songs couldn't be played until the two-hour mark: Guns N' Roses' "Paradise City," the Rolling Stones' "Sympathy for the Devil," and especially "Free Bird." These were all over six minutes long, and if they were whipped out too soon, they could stall the evening's momentum. The one exception to this rule was "Stairway to Heaven," which was not to be played under any circumstances whatsoever.

• During Temple of the Dog's "Hunger Strike," the group in the room had to be divided in half, with one side singing Eddie Vedder's part, and the other tackling Chris Cornell's part.

• Everyone had to clap during Hall & Oates's "Private Eyes," including the puppets. *Especially* the puppets.

Let me explain the puppets.

During the summer of 2000, Mike and I created a Manhattan public-access television show called *Karaoke! Adventure!* It aired Fridays at 11 P.M., and to best of my knowledge, its audience consisted of one kid at Columbia who accidentally saw it twice. I'd occasionally meet people who were impressed by the fact that we had a TV show, even though getting a slot on Manhattan Neighborhood Network was easy: All you had to do was film something that wasn't snuff or hardcore pornography, convert it to VHS, and drop it off at the MNN offices once every two weeks. If you could manage that—and there were weeks when we couldn't—you'd get a time slot somewhere between *Astoria Psychic* and *Black Kids Playing Videogames.*

In its six-episode span, *Karaoke! Adventure!* rarely followed through on any of its titular promises. The karaoke footage was shaky and incomplete, and the so-called "adventures" were long, noticeably unscripted sketches that starred a bunch of low-budget animal puppets we'd purchased in a toy store. The puppets weren't included with any grand creative intent; they were simply goofy-looking and cheap, and sometimes, there's nothing more enjoyable than getting drunk and manipulating a googley-eyed piece of cloth. Considering that the most recurring character on *Karaoke! Adventure!* was a chain-smoking frog who sang H-Town's "Knockin' Da Boots," I'd like to think Mike and I pioneered the sort of drunken, unfunny shit now commonly found on YouTube.

When we tired of Village Karaoke's technical difficulties or long lines, we'd occasionally investigate other karaoke venues, few of which offered the sort of slipshod kicks found in our Bowery home. Two especially precarious excursions both took place on the same summer trip to Long Island, where the sing-along options were limited: The first stop was the Memory Motel, a dive bar in Montauk immortalized in a 1976 song by the Rolling Stones. I picked Van Halen's "Jump," and because I wanted to pay proper homage to David Lee Roth's original vocal stylings, my performance mostly consisted of yelling *waahh-ohhh* and/or *waa-ooooh* over and over again. This did not go over too well with one of the townies sitting at the bar, who glared at me the rest of the evening until I lobbied that we go elsewhere.

A few days later, we found ourselves at a fancy gay nightclub that was hosting a *Gong Show*–style karaoke contest, though the gong was a trashcan lid, and Chuck Barris was a surly drag queen. My friend Kevin signed up to sing first, which surprised me: I'd known him since we were about five years old, and when he was younger, he was more interested in sports than music. Yet here he was, jumping around in a gay Hamptons nightclub while wearing a tight-fitting green T-shirt that read "IRISH," singing the Proclaimers' "500 Miles." When the drag queen finally bashed the trash-can lid, Kevin looked relieved, and not at all disappointed. The first 50 miles or so had been more than enough excitement for the night.

Mike and I were up next, and I needed multiple shots of vodka before taking the mic, mostly because I was intimidated by the club's in-the-round seating; it was packed with men, a giant gay thunderdome. We sang the Human League's "Don't You Want Me Baby" and made it all the way through, much to my surprise.

"So, are you guys a couple?" the host asked us during our post-performance Q&A.

"A couple of fools!" I replied, perhaps a tad defensively.

We were immediately gonged, victims of blatant heterophobia. But even on this night, like all the others, we wound up singing out on the streets afterward, so loud that anyone behind us could see the cartoon clef notes zipping above our heads.

☙

Because Mike filmed many of our early karaoke shindigs, I have my first year in New York caught on tape, and the footage is excruciating to watch. I made two strategic mistakes during that time: The first was initiating a near-daily ritual in which I began every day with a buttered bagel and a can of Orange Sunkist, and finished each night with a trip to the Times Square Pizza Hut. The second mistake was enrolling in Supercuts' buy-twelve-get-one-free scheme. Anyone who saw those *Karaoke! Adventure!* episodes would be forgiven for thinking that I was a porcupine who'd learned to pass among humans by wearing khaki pants.

Yet there are moments in that footage in which I'm singing to the entire group, and that's when I look the most relaxed, even if just for a few seconds. When I went to parties, I pinned myself against the wall, out of view; but inside the karaoke rooms, I stood on the table, welcoming the cameras and the attention, knowing every word. Karaoke induced a sort of time-release euphoria, one that flatlined my anxieties and allowed me to float high above the room. When I looked down at myself, I'd see cracks of self-confidence and wonder where they went during the rest of the week, when I actually needed them. I was a different person when I sang, and after a year of Village Karaoke, I decided to see if I could be that person all the time.

This required me to drastically alter my karaoke lifestyle. In need of clarity, I stopped drinking for a few months, and even learned to perform while stone-cold sober—which is actually easy to do, so long as everyone else is drunk. After a while, I realized that it wasn't the alcohol or the puppetry that gave me this assurance; it was the fact that these people accepted—and even encouraged—the very weirdness that had made me feel so out of place for so long. They emboldened me, and in the spring of 2000, I resolved to finally lose all the weight I'd been accruing over the past decade. I got up early every day and went to the gym, where I sang along with Def Leppard on the treadmill. And I scaled back my hot dog intake, from eight a week to merely two. In a few months, I lost nearly 20 pounds—it all just slid off, as though it was never supposed to be there in the first place.

One night, not so long after I lost that weight, I brought a girl to one of our Village Karaoke parties. I'd only known her for a few weeks, and I was a little too crazy for her, as I'd soon find out with a polite but firmly dismissive phone call. But on that Saturday we kissed on the sidewalk, in an exchange that I'd been expecting for weeks but waiting for since high school: *Finally, a hot girl likes the way I sing.*

None of this, I knew, would have happened if not for karaoke. So I said goodnight and went in to sing for another two hours.

CHAPTER 2

The Emulation Nation

DURING OUR FIRST FEW YEARS IN NEW YORK CITY, IT SEEMED AS THOUGH MY FRIENDS AND I HAD VILLAGE KARAOKE TO OURSELVES. While there were always a few drunken NYU students or homesick Japanese tourists hanging around, it was never that difficult to get a room. And even if we did stop by on a busy night, we could always count on Koji—a Japanese student who worked the front door—to wave us past the line and find us a spot. In exchange for this V.I.P. treatment, we always snuck Koji into our room for a quick hit of Stevie Wonder's "Isn't She Lovely?" After performing it in his heavily accented lilt, Koji would run back to the front desk, where he'd flip over half a dozen or so laser discs, therefore saving us all from another karaoke-queue implosion.

Around the fall of 2002, however, I began hearing more voices at Village Karaoke—voices that slipped out of open doorways and twisted down the hall, where they became one noisy, tangled echo. Rooms that were once empty now required a waiting list, and if we wanted to sing on the weekend, we had to plan ahead and call Koji, who sounded increasingly harried on the other line.

If he happened to be off for the night, we'd loiter around the desk, hoping to talk our way into a room and listening to the constant *waughhh* of the front-door buzzer—a reminder of Village Karaoke's newfound popularity.

I didn't mind the crowds, as it meant more opportunities for us to run from room to room, surprising our neighbors with random outbursts of third-rate puppetry. Though Mike and I had long stopped producing new episodes of *Karaoke! Adventure!*, the karaoke parties continued, and the puppets were still in attendance, albeit worse for the wear. Years of spilled drinks and cigarette smoke had given their fur a horrible stench, so before we went out for the night, Mike and I held their plush carcasses at arm's length and hosed them down with Glade. I imagine this is not unlike being married to Peter O'Toole.

After spending so much of the early 2000s trying to cajole friends and coworkers into making the trek downtown, I was confounded to see that Village Karaoke had become an actual destination. Surely, the people waiting in line with us had better things to do on a Friday night than hang around a karaoke joint. Where had they come from? And, more importantly, what was bringing them here?

What I didn't know at the time was that America was in the throes of a karaoke revolution. When the first sing-along devices were introduced here in the early '80s, they were viewed as a sort of novelty toy, one headed for swift and certain obsolescence. Even when karaoke proved to be commercially viable in the '90s, it remained an object of ridicule, championed by a few die-hards, but sneered at or ignored by everyone else. This began to change in the late '90s, thanks to a series of cultural and demographic shifts that forever altered the public's perception of karaoke. The long waits at Village Karaoke were indicative of what was happening around the country, where karaoke was experiencing a sudden surge in popularity, with bars and nightclubs adding specialized karaoke nights, and young consumers buying up low-priced, high-tech karaoke machines they could use at home. By 2004, it was possible for a movie like *Lost in Translation*—which featured a karaoke-room dalliance—to be nominated for multiple Oscars, and for Democratic activists to launch nationwide "Kerryoke" nights. After years of being kept at a distance, karaoke was no longer America's smelly puppet. It had finally gone legit, and all thanks to the combined efforts of a few million excitable teenagers, a few dozen patient businessmen, and one ungodly popular television show.

To anyone who's ever waited for hours for their turn at a karaoke bar—or who's watched the audition footage that pads out shows like *American Idol* and *Rock Star* and *My Groundskeeper Can Rap*—it's hard to imagine a time when Americans *didn't* want to make public spectacles of themselves. But for the businessmen trying to break karaoke wide in the '80s, convincing even one person to sing could be a major hassle. Ernie Taylor, the founder of a Los Angeles karaoke-supply wholesaler named Trax, describes his earliest attempts to lure people to karaoke with frustration. Taylor was a piano salesman when he saw his first karaoke machine at a consumer electronics convention in 1983, and because he loved to sing, he assumed the public would be as enthusiastic about the device as he was. And yet, "there was resistance on the part of the clubs to put it in," Taylor says now. "And there was resistance from the people themselves to get up and sing. People couldn't get over the idea that *they* could be part of the entertainment, rather than sitting in the audience and [allowing] the experts to perform for them. It took a long time to educate the public."

David Bellagamba, an Orlando-based entrepreneur, encountered the same obstacles when he began booking karaoke parties in his hometown in the late '80s. After promoting everything from disco concerts to male-stripper revues, Bellagamba was well aware of the public's erratic tastes. But even he was surprised by the difficulties he encountered getting karaoke machines into the bars and restaurants along Orlando's touristy International Drive area. "Nobody would open the door for us," he says. "Owners said, 'People won't do this. They won't sing.'" Even when he did manage to land a karaoke gig, Bellagamba sometimes wound up serving as the evening's entertainment, often against his own wishes. "I was hustling people in the audience—'Come on, let's do a duet together.' That was the story of my life for a long time."

To many Americans, karaoke was nothing but a queerly named import. There'd been nothing quite like it in U.S. culture, and it was mysterious and untested—something to be feared. It didn't help that the media often treated karaoke with skepticism or outright contempt. I've read numerous wacky-trend feature stories on karaoke from the '80s and '90s, many of which take the same half-bemused, half-offended tone evident in this 1993 article from the *Atlanta Journal-Constitution*:

> They are braying like mules in Marietta, taking songs like "My Way" and "Mack the Knife" in directions Ol' Blue Eyes never intended. . . .
>
>   It's called karaoke, and if you haven't heard it yet, it's clear you're deaf. But at more than 100 locations in and around Atlanta each week, patrons line up to stand in front of a roomful of strangers and sing, sing, sing. The music is canned and the electronically cued lyrics appear on a video

screen, but the voices are real, and it's a horrible, awful racket that's as entertaining as it is bad. . . .

Why would self-respecting human beings willingly humiliate themselves like this in public, especially in front of people who may or may not be their friends? Have they no pride?

That's an especially disdainful example, but it illustrates the way in which many cultural observers viewed karaoke—as a jokey oddity, one that was undeserving of closer examination, no matter how many people might enjoy it. Even the word itself became tainted, such as when George H.W. Bush referred to Bill Clinton and Al Gore as "the karaoke kids" during a 1992 campaign speech. The comment was intended as a dig at their flip-flopping on issues—"they'll sing any tune they think will get them elected," Bush said—and even though the joke didn't make a lot of sense, he'd hung the word on Clinton and Gore. It was as if the mere suggestion of karaoke was enough to demean them.

Those who worked in the karaoke industry were aware of this stigma, so much so that Pioneer, an electronics company that produced many of the early karaoke laser discs, once created a print ad in which a kid recoils from his father's singing. The copy on the ad reads, "Trouble getting your kids to leave?" But it may as well have said, "Karaoke: So fucking annoying that it will make your kid resent you more than usual." Even one of the many karaoke-industry veterans I interviewed for the book told me that, despite making a tidy income from producing instrumental tracks, he and many of his colleagues considered karaoke to be "cute, but kinda cheesy."

But why was the simple act of singing in front of others met with such resistance? Certainly, many people were put off by the alien-sounding word, which nobody knew how to pronounce (it's car-OH-kay, not carrie-OH-key, though the Japanese have long given up on convincing us otherwise). And it didn't help that early karaoke technology allowed for a limited selection of songs. But I think the opposition toward karaoke was rooted in fear—the fear of looking untalented or uncool, of demeaning yourself in a public setting. And for this, I don't blame standard-issue American social hang-ups. I blame Bill Murray.

In 1977, Murray debuted one of his most popular *Saturday Night Live* characters, an undeservedly cocksure lounge singer named Nick. Whether he was headlining at a ski lodge (as Nick Winters) or a Hawaiian-themed lounge (as Nick Lava), Murray's creation always interpreted the hits of the day, often incorrectly. He turned Bob Dylan's "You Gotta Serve Somebody" into a plea for better tips, and added lyrics to the *Star Wars* theme ("If they should bar wars/please let the *Star Wars*/stayyyy"). Musically and socially, Nick was a bore, unaware that his audience of feuding couples, drunken hunters, and philandering spouses preferred to be left alone. Yet Nick never let them be. He stuck microphones in their faces and made idiotic segues (in one bit, he talked about the prom-night car-crash that killed his girlfriend and then launched into an upbeat piano version of "Stairway to Heaven"). Nick was perfectly dunderheaded, the sort of enduring comedy character that inspired Monday-morning homeroom recitals and became a staple of *SNL* best-of compilations.

The Nick sketches weren't intended as a parody of karaoke, as Murray was accompanied by Paul Shaffer on piano, and besides, karaoke was still mostly unheard of in America in the late '70s. But Murray's hepcat-hack character became a cultural archetype. When I was younger, I'd walk by a cocktail lounge and see a black-and-white headshot on the door—usually some guy with a lone arched eyebrow and an open-collar dress shirt—and instantly hear that butchered *Star Wars* jingle. It didn't matter that I'd never even seen the inside of a karaoke bar, or *any* bar, for that matter. As far as I was concerned, they were full of Nick-types, one great big cornball chorus.

Much in the same way that Nurse Ratchet became America's go-to insane-asylum nurse, or Cliff Clavin its resident sad-sack mailman, Nick's cultural omnipresence made him our go-to tacky crooner. And because the dimly lit, cavernous cocktail bars where Nick thrived weren't too far removed from some of the karaoke bars of the '80s and '90s, it's safe to assume that when people thought of karaoke, they thought of Nick. In popular culture, sometimes the exaggerator creates the exemplar.

The early resistance to karaoke wasn't all Murray's fault, of course. But the sketches hit upon a fear that many people have about karaoke—namely, that of looking like a grandly unaware schmuck. Nobody wanted to be like Nick, and this may be why so many films portray karaoke as a potentially traumatizing endeavor. It's why Billy Crystal looks so mortified when his ex catches him using a karaoke machine in *When Harry Met Sally;* why Julia Roberts forces her rival Cameron Diaz to sing "I Just Don't Know What to Do with Myself" at a karaoke bar in *My Best Friend's Wedding;* and why Jennifer Love Hewitt doesn't want to sing in front of her friends in *I Still Know What You Did Last Summer.* In all of these scenes, it's assumed that audiences will understand the inherent danger of karaoke: public humiliation. That threat underscores the comic tension, and for a long time, Nick's atonal ghost hovered in the background of all karaoke bars, whether on the screen or in the real world.

Though its credibility was no doubt damaged by chortling newspaper accounts and various cultural stigmas, karaoke nonetheless managed to survive. What its supporters lacked in numbers, they made up for with enthusiasm, and throughout the early '90s, as bars across America began holding weekly karaoke nights, many of its critics learned to accept karaoke, even if they did so begrudgingly. Now, more than twenty years since it got its start in America, karaoke enjoys a sort of cultural centrism: It's not exactly cool, but it's not exactly *uncool* either. Karaoke remains a bit weird, and certainly grandma-confusing, but few of its remaining critics can really bother to get all worked up about it anymore. To make fun of karaoke now would be about as timely and relevant as making fun of Marilyn Quayle's pillbox hats. And the trepidation about being dragged onto a karaoke stage has diminished greatly as well. Lenny Morheim, a Long Island–based retailer of karaoke machines since 1983, says the era in which promoters had to beg for singers has long since passed. "Nowadays, if you go out on a gig, the KJ doesn't have time to sing, because the mic is hogged all night," he says. "The bashfulness is gone. They don't care if they sound good." This is a major cultural shift, one I attribute to three key turn-of-the-century events:

1. *May 18, 1999: The Backstreet Boys release* Millennium

For a three-year period that began with the issuing of *Millennium* (which sold 12 million copies) and ended with the November 11, 2002, release of O-Town's *02* (which did not sell anywhere near 12 million copies), radio and MTV were steered by the erratic whims of a moppet cabal. The music charts were dominated by the likes of Britney Spears, *NSYNC, and the Backstreet Boys, all of whom worked out of a secret Swedish laboratory, recording songs with simplistic yet elephantine hooks. "It was like going back to the '60s, with better production values," notes Ed Pearson, who's been marketing and developing karaoke equipment since 1991. "It's all three-chord songs that anybody can sing." *Millennium* included the era's high-watermark hit, "I Want It That Way," a ballad with lyrics about fire and desire, not to mention an unforgettable "Tell me why-eee" chorus. At a time when rock radio had become so Neolithic—the 2000 album chart featured Limp Bizkit, Creed, and Papa Roach—a song like "That Way" had great power. It was light and accessible, and seemingly created to be enjoyed en masse. The same can be said for such tracks as *NSYNC's "Bye Bye Bye," Christina Aguilera's "What a Girl Wants," and just about any non-ballad released by Britney Spears from 1999 to 2003.

This was not the first musical youth movement to occur in the karaoke era. Between 1987 and 1989, the country's best-selling albums included Tiffany's *Tiffany,* Deborah Gibson's *Out of the Blue,* and New Kids on the Block's *Hangin' Tough.* The songs produced during this period were no less addictive and participatory than those from the late '90s, and to this day, Gibson's "Only in My Dreams" and the New Kids' "(You Got It) The Right Stuff"—which include, respectively, 30 backing *ahh*s and 112 backing *oooh*s—make for stellar karaoke numbers. But in 2000, there were more than 31 million teens in America—an increase of 4.5 million since 1990, according to a study by Teenage Research Unlimited, a research firm that defines teenager as anyone between twelve and nineteen years old. These kids were living with a vibrant economy, and they were willing to spend their money on anything. Even a subprime boy-band like 98 Degrees could sell 4 million copies of an album, and those guys were little more than overgroomed remoras picking the detritus from Lou Pearlman's great white underbelly. Between 1999 and 2002, *every* song was a hit song, and hit songs draw people to karaoke.

For those in the karaoke industry, the timing of teen-pop couldn't have been better. The earliest karaoke machines were introduced in the '80s and ran as high as $2,000. But with the advent of an early '90s technology called CD+G (for compact disc and graphics), it was now possible to put minimally designed videos onto cheaply produced discs; as a result, karaoke machines became inexpensive and portable, some of them no bigger than a boombox. Instead of waiting until they were old enough to go to a bar, teenagers could now sing at home, and stores such as Target and Wal-Mart carried CD+G compilations of Britney and Christina. Even MTV entered the marketplace, putting its logo on an $80 machine that was created to fit into tote bags and backpacks (a Nickelodeon line soon followed).

But teen-pop did more than just sell a few extra karaoke machines. It minted an entirely new generation of music enthusiasts, one populated by kids who'd grown up under the thumb of Disney culture—from *The Lion King* and *Aladdin* to Radio Disney—and who were now watching as their all-singing, some-dancing peers dominated the popular culture. The music of the period was psychotically chipper, and often performed by singers with little natural singing ability: I'd describe Jessica Simpson's voice as "robotic," but I imagine that would make most robots sad. Yet Simpson's fans didn't mind—it was her personality that was being sold, not her talent, and all that really mattered was that she made singing look incredibly fun. To her fans, "cute, but kinda cheesy" wasn't an insult. It was a lifestyle.

This was radically different from my own teenage experience, during which the musical iconography was made up of sourpusses like Eddie Vedder, Kurt Cobain, and Ian MacKaye. When I was in high school, you only sang if you had something absolutely important to say, or if you had an exceptional voice, which was one of the reasons why I'd been so reluctant to try karaoke at first. I knew that, with my voice, I had no business being on a stage, and I was afraid I'd look like one of those unaware lounge-singer twits. Yet the teen-pop disciples had no such qualms. They hadn't grown up with the foreboding memory of Nick Lava, but with the middling reality of Nick Lachey, whose pandering sentiment and wrung-out vocals were just as pronounced as Murray's, though presumably less ironic. The stigma of being a not-so-great singer (and of being proven so at karaoke) was gone.

2. September 4, 2002: The season-one finale of American Idol *is watched by nearly 23 million people*

When *Idol* premiered in June 2002, the first thing I noticed was how non-insane most of the contestants looked. While most music-competition TV shows were dominated by stage-mothered brats, the *Idol* hopefuls appeared grateful and eager to please, like members of an especially attentive Shoney's waitstaff. I didn't miss an episode of that first season, mostly because I felt like I was witnessing a major change within the entertainment industry. By loading the show with personal-narrative backstory and "candid" footage, Fox sold the public on the idea that these contestants (which included ex-waitresses, ex-telemarketers, and even an ex-stripper) were no different from the rest of us. When viewers saw Kelly Clarkson, a twenty-year-old former Red Bull salesgirl who said "y'all" a lot, they saw a favorite niece or a former babysitter, or maybe even themselves. This was the underlying appeal of the show's first season: that musical talent could be found anywhere, and that mere commoners could succeed through a meritocracy. It didn't matter that some of these contestants were actually show-business veterans, or that their voices were uncommonly superhuman—Clarkson, for example, had a vibrato that sounded like God's car alarm. They seemed relatable, and even though that was just an illusion, it was empowering. And maybe a bit subversive.

One of the reasons we worship talent is that it appears to be a preexisting condition—a singular achievement that could never be duplicated. The traditional artist-audience paradigm dictates that performers are to be elevated above the rest of us, as they do something that we cannot; our role is to merely gape. But *Idol*'s celebration of complete nobodies—albeit nobodies who'd already secured representation—suggested that those of us who were in the audience could be just as talented as the people on stage, even if we didn't know it. I don't think the show's producers actually believed this, as evidenced by their glee in broadcasting the second season's lesser-skilled applicants, an unnecessary and mean-spirited move that allowed the show to offer up William Hung as a sacrificial ham. Yet even if the show's you-can-do-it spirit was just a cynical marketing ploy, it changed the way that many viewers related to popular culture: After all, if Kelly Clarkson can make it, why can't you? Wouldn't it at least be fun to try?

The cultural reversal wrought by *Idol* has introduced a new paradigm, one in which the audience members *become* the artist. Sometimes this happens almost literally, such as when Jordin Sparks—who was twelve years old when she watched Clarkson's 2002 *Idol* victory—made repeated try-outs for the show before being crowned the winner in 2007. But often, it's done in an imitative manner. In November 2005, Activision introduced *Guitar Hero,* a video game in which users manipulate a banjo-sized plastic guitar to play hits like Deep Purple's "Smoke on the Water" and Franz Ferdinand's "Take Me Out." No actual musical skills are needed for the game; in fact, it's possible to play with the music turned all the way off, simply by following along with the visual cues. Yet it's not unusual to hear fans of *Guitar Hero*—and its multi-instrument sequel, *Rock Band*—equating their virtual-world skills with real-world skills, as though the act of punching a few buttons in a predetermined sequence is akin to reading and performing music. This is partly because *Guitar Hero* approximates what it feels like to be a rock star—or rather, what we *think* it must feel like. But another reason for the game's success is that in the post-*Idol* era, musical talent has been reduced to a commodity. It's something that can be dissected, replicated, mass-manufactured, and ultimately consumed.

This is the show's ultimate legacy, one that can be most keenly observed in America's many overcrowded karaoke bars. Nearly every karaoke-industry veteran I interviewed agreed that *Idol* has played a role in karaoke's increased popularity, despite the show's judges occasionally employing "karaoke" as code for "shitshow." "It didn't throw roses at us," says Morheim, the Long Island karaoke distributor, "but it did make the word 'karaoke' more visible." It also reminded viewers who were too old for that teen-pop boom that singing was an immensely pleasurable act: *Idol* contestants were twentysomething kids who could have been home playing Xbox or watching *Alias*, and instead they were singing forty-year-old Mamas and the Papas songs as if they were the *most exciting thing in the whole world.* During that first season, it was almost impossible not to play along at home, and I suspect many of those who did later turned to karaoke. *Idol* was a reminder of the joys of creating music, even if you were just following along. It spawned knock-off shows like *Celebrity Duets* and *Rock Star: INXS*, and it's the reason why every alt-weekly I pick up in every city I visit advertises some sort of karaoke competition with the word "Idol" in the title. It validated the amateur.

3. October 3, 2003: Nick the Lounge Singer dies, and Bill Murray is redeemed

In *Lost in Translation,* Bill Murray plays Bob Harris, an American movie star who travels to Japan to shoot an ad for Suntory whiskey. He's also fleeing from a stilted marriage back home:

When his wife calls him long-distance to discuss the carpet-tile samples she's considering for their home, Harris slides into the tub, defeated. While sitting in his hotel bar, miserable with insomnia, he meets Charlotte (Scarlett Johansson), a fellow tourist who has an inattentive husband and a useless philosophy degree. She's also having trouble sleeping, so the two of them decide to explore Tokyo at night, and while at a k-box, they subtly woo each other with karaoke. Charlotte vamps around in a shocking-pink wig and sings the Pretenders' "Brass in Pocket," while he performs an earnest version of Roxy Music's "More Than This."

The k-box sequence is only a few minutes long, and yet it's the most accurate depiction of karaoke I've ever seen on film, one that's filled with familiar details. There's the songbook splayed out on Murray's lap; the artless room, decorated with nothing but a cheap lighting rig; and the awkward sound equipment, which reduces the backing track to a wisp and exposes the vocals. And while Murray does engage in a wild-man version of Elvis Costello's "(What's So Funny 'Bout) Peace, Love, and Understanding," the scene isn't played for laughs; the quick glances shared by Charlotte and Bob during "More Than This" are genuine. No smugness, no ironic detachment. The lounge-lizard is extinct.

Karaoke was already becoming de-weirded by the time of *Translation*'s release, but the movie proved that a karaoke bar was a place where one could sing what couldn't be said—where a few lines of an old Roxy Music tune could express a connection that couldn't be voiced in any other way. The idea of karaoke-room flirtation had previously been explored in the 2000 romantic drama *Duets*, which finds yet another middle-aged man (Paul Giamatti) in the throes of a midlife crisis, one that prompts him to leave his wife and cozy up to a young karaoke-bar patron. But Giamatti's character is so cartoonishly overwritten—he goes from being a meek salesman to a gun-toting, ear-pierced maniac—that the movie never once feels grounded in reality. *Translation* is *all* reality. It's to karaoke what *Watchmen* is to comic books—a redemptive tribute for longtime devotees, and the perfect entry point for nonbelievers. After the film's success, I didn't have to explain to people what a k-box was, or justify my time spent inside one.

The combination of *American Idol, Lost in Translation,* and the teen-pop movement may have provided the country with a permission slip to sing, but the mainstream approval of karaoke had an unintended side effect: It killed Village Karaoke.

I should have seen it coming, but to be honest, by 2005 my friends and I weren't paying much attention to Village Karaoke anymore. Koji had returned to Japan, and once he was gone, we no longer had access to the generous room-rate discounts and preferred treatment. When you're suddenly paying full price for a room, the faulty equipment becomes a lot less endearing. And after several years of abuse, Village Karaoke's rooms had gone from slightly ramshackle to borderline derelict. There were holes in the walls, duct-tape patches had appeared on the furniture, and the intra-room phones were dead. At one point, a friend of mine rented a room with a few of his coworkers, and as they sang, a giant rat scurried across the floor. Knowing Village Karaoke, the rat had probably picked a song two hours earlier and was still waiting for it to come on.

The clientele, meanwhile, had gotten rowdier, so much so that the owners finally hired a bouncer. But his main task seemed to be discouraging underage drinkers from abusing Village's BYOB policy, and he couldn't prevent people from emptying the fire extinguisher into the hallway or clogging the toilets with paper towels. There were also rumors of customers having sex in the rooms, though, considering that the doors had diamond-shaped windows, I can't imagine anyone being pantsless for more than one song without getting caught.

In the end, what ultimately doomed Village Karaoke—at least for me—was the sudden influx of karaoke competition. It wasn't just the new karaoke bars in the East Village, or the refurbished private rooms in Koreatown. There were karaoke nights opening up all over the city, sometimes with a live band. Village Karaoke tried to keep up, adding new songs and improving its hardware, but Mike and I had already migrated to another Lower East Side bar called Sing Sing, which had a deeper song selection and shorter waits. After the karaoke revolution, my friends and I could sing anywhere, and the very qualities that had made Village Karaoke so desirable in the first place—its punk-rock vibe, its indifference to modernity—suddenly made it seem like a throwback.

I don't remember the last time I went to Village Karaoke; I just know that, at some point, I realized it had been about six months since my last visit, and then a year, and then even longer. There were persistent rumors of its demise, but whenever I called to ask, the person on the other line would deny this and quickly hang up.

One night, I walked by and noticed that the storefront's neon sign was out. "Maybe it's shut down for the night," I thought, even though I knew that Village Karaoke *never* shut down for the night. A few weeks later, I returned to find the doors boarded up. Signs posted to the windows promised a brand-new luxury hotel, coming soon. I stood on the sidewalk for a few moments, regretting the fact that I'd never given the place a proper send-off, and cursing myself for never stealing one of its dollar-store disco-light machines as a memento. But I didn't mourn Village Karaoke for long.

In the end, it was only a karaoke bar, one that had lived far longer than it should have.

Still, there are nights when I get into the back of a Manhattan cab, eager to go somewhere familiar, yet not quite ready to go home. And as the driver looks into the mirror for instructions, I instinctively want to say, "Bowery, between Fifth and Sixth."

Adventures in Karaoke

Fleetwood Mac, "Dreams"
March 26, 2004
Tokyo, Japan

We're knee-deep in the water, singing Justin Timberlake's "Rock Your Body," when we find out the hot-tub girls won't be joining us. It's an early evening in Tokyo, and Mike, Kevin, and I are in a luxury karaoke suite above the city's glossy Roppongi district, a neighborhood that appears to have been zoned exclusively for prodigal consumerism. Our room costs about $100 an hour and includes a white-walled hot tub, a high-definition monitor, and a changing area stocked with three pairs of pressed floral-print bathing suits. As I wade into the tub wearing my bathrobe, I have a beer mug in one hand and a wireless microphone in the other. We have the option of ordering food as well, but I don't want to eat in the tub. That would be tacky.

The absence of hot-tub girls is dispiriting, but not for the reasons you might think. When we signed up for the room, we were told that a few of the female employees might be stopping by for a song or two. So far as we could tell, it wasn't a sexual thing, which was fine by us—after nearly a week together in Japan, the three of us would have enjoyed *any* outside intervention, even if it consisted of nothing more than a barely intelligible back-and-forth on the merits of Justin Timberlake. This was our third international trip together, and the intensity of day-to-day life in Japan—which required perpetual motion and stifling proximity—had introduced some minor strain: Since Kevin was not as fanatical about karaoke as Mike and I were, I could tell he was growing weary of being tugged toward a new karaoke bar every night. And because Mike could whisk through the city on just a few hours' sleep, he was no doubt sick of his traveling companions' inability to stay in a Japanese arcade until 4 A.M. every night.

As for me, I was so intolerably distant and moody that the two of them would have been justified in doping me with chloroform, wrapping me in a hotel rug, and placing me in the cargo hold of a Nagasaki bullet train. In the spring of 2004, I was suffering through a protracted breakup, the kind that turns common household objects into shrines and friends into unwilling therapists. For nearly two years, I'd been dating a woman whose many outstanding traits included a love of karaoke. During the day, we worked together at *Entertainment Weekly,* where we talked about bad movies and keytars; at night, we sat on a park bench in Brooklyn, drinking red wine out of a coffee thermos. And whenever we had a chance, we'd find a place to sing. Once, while staying in a Montreal hotel room, I became so tipsily consumed with an old Phil Collins tune that she had to call the concierge, declaring a "karaoke emergency" in our room. Within a few minutes, we were in a cab heading toward a karaoke bar, where I serenaded my girlfriend and the two other customers with "Against All Odds (Take a Look at Me Now)."

But it had ended, in part because I was still so unformed when it came to relationships, and too inexperienced to realize that stubbornness isn't always an admirable trait. I wasn't ready for her. And now, realizing that it was truly finished, I couldn't go more than a minute without being fatigued with regret. So I did what depressive insomniacs always do in such situations: I went to the other end of the world.

To keep myself distracted during the trip, I'd managed to convince my new bosses at *GQ* magazine to turn the vacation into an assignment. *Lost in Translation* had just been released, and I pitched a story on trying to find the best karaoke bar in Tokyo. Because of my state of mind, I'd become lazy and indifferent toward my job, and this was the first good idea I'd had in months: Not only would I be going somewhere with absolutely no geographical ties to my failed relationship, but I'd finally be visiting the karaoke motherland. Plus, I'd be able to put hundreds of dollars of karaoke on a corporate card.

The problems began almost as soon as we arrived in Tokyo. We walked straight from our hotel to a karaoke room, where I indulged myself on *nomihoodai*, which managed to keep me in a deceptively elated state until we got back to our hotel. While Mike and Kevin slept, I stared at the overworked neon outside my window and constantly checked an international cell phone that I'd borrowed from the magazine, just in case my ex decided to call me and get back together. No matter how many Ambiens I took, I could only get two or three hours of sleep at a time, and during the day, as we walked around temples and ancient dojos, I remained in a selfish stupor, either not talking at all or just waiting to steer the conversation back to me. I felt like a sham, working at a men's magazine that espoused the virtues of being an unapologetic lady-killer, yet unable to get over a relationship that was three months gone.

It was only during our karaoke sessions that I'd get a reprieve, as if my serotonin levels were directly related to the number of Wings songs I could perform. So we did karaoke all the time, and as aggressively as possible. The Japanese songbooks were like the documents of some alternative pop-music universe—one in which Mr. Big has just as many hits as the Beatles. Every night, we found dozens of elusive songs, many of which I'd wanted to sing for years but could never find back home, like Weezer's "Surf Wax America" and Ace Frehley's "New York Groove." Oddly, the only track I *couldn't* locate in Japan was "Godzilla," the 1977 Blue Oyster Cult song that combines heavy metal from the states and bipedal monsters from the sea, two of Japan's long-running cultural obsessions. Not finding the song there was strange—like showing up at a steel mill in western Pennsylvania and discovering that no one wanted to sing "Allentown."

But even the 200-page songbooks could only distract me for so long, and by the end of the week, I was feeling even worse than I had back home. Nearly a whole week had passed, and the inbox on my overpriced cell phone was empty. As we sat in the hot tub that night, I performed completely on autopilot, as if all the lyrics (and their accompanying dance moves) were on a preset timer. I even faked my way through "Rock Your Body," which is hard to do, as it requires slight beat-boxing. That night, I got back to the hotel and drank myself to sleep.

The next morning, during our last day of the trip, Mike and Kevin decided to go shopping, leaving me to fend for myself in the neighborhood around our hotel. In Tokyo, karaoke bars enjoy a block-by-block ubiquity that matches Dublin's pubs and Manhattan's bodegas, and as I scouted the catacombs of electronics stores and noodle shops, I looked for the now-familiar Japanese script for "empty orchestra":

カラオケ

I eventually found a k-box joint advertising an early-afternoon *nomihoodai* special, so I put my credit card down on the counter and pointed repeatedly at the sign, which is the U.N.-recognized code for, "I am a foreigner who will never, ever understand your weird-looking receipts, so please just charge whatever you'd like, as I'll be too humiliated to dispute it three months from now." Shortly afterward, I was escorted to my own private room, where I was given a pitcher of beer and a demonstration of how to use the elaborate remote control.

I stayed in the room for an hour, drinking and smoking, and singing nothing but '70s soft-rock numbers (plus Hole's "Malibu," which is essentially a '70s soft-rock number with distortion). The bar had almost every track from Fleetwood Mac's *Rumours*, an album that seemed appropriate for my situation, as it was the result of several doomed workplace relationships. When I finally got to "Dreams," I closed my eyes and recited the lyrics by heart:

> *Well, there you go again*
> *You say you want your freedom*

Those words aren't mine, of course; they were written by Stevie Nicks, in reference to whichever Fleetwood Mac member she was dating at the time. But as I sat in that room by myself, the words became mine: It was as though Stevie and I were collaborating, and only the two of us understood what it was like to experience this very keen sort of heartbreak. Music lovers, even passive ones, often talk about being able to relate to a certain song, but at karaoke, you can actually *inhabit* that song and make it your own.

The last few months had been not only upsetting for me, but confounding—I couldn't connect with anyone around me, and didn't know how to express what I was feeling. For those few minutes of "Dreams," I wasn't at a loss for words.

So, if you happen to be Stevie Nicks: Thanks.

When my time was up, I went back to my hotel and packed for the flight home. I went back to New York City with an empty voice-mail queue and a bill for more than $1,100 worth of karaoke. I left *GQ* a few months later, and the story never ran.

CHAPTER 3

Heavy Metal Memories

A MONDAY NIGHT ON THE LOWER EAST SIDE, CIRCA 1999:

What the fuck am I doing?

There are 300 people here, easily. Maybe 500. And they're almost all girls—rocker girls with old Mötley Crüe concert T-shirts, which are probably real vintage shirts, not shopping-mall knock-offs. Jesus, these girls are foxy. Authentically *foxy. Who gets to date these kinds of girls? Investment bankers? Firemen?*

I should say something funny.

I think the bassist is scowling at me. Since when does a bassist get the right to scowl? Is this what happens when a band doesn't have a real singer?

Oof.

They're starting to play. This song is only two minutes long, so maybe I can make it through if I just scream the whole time. I'll scream the words and close

my eyes, and when it's over, I will step over the heads of
all of these people and run ass-crazy into the street like
Martin Lawrence. And just so no one will ever make me
do this again, I'll keep this fear with me at all times, for
reference.

   This is the end of my life.

Between 1999 and 2001, I made several weekly trips to Arlene's
Grocery, a Manhattan club with exposed-brick walls, a few candle-
lit tables, and a trifling stage that felt more like a plank than a performance area. This was the home of the Original Punk
Rock/Heavy Metal Karaoke Band, a trio that played Clash and
Quiet Riot songs but left the vocals to the audience members—an
excitable lot that included head-bangers, squares, lawyers, jazz
musicians, expat-frat boys, and the occasional guido. Every Monday night, they'd gather at Arlene's, where, one by one, they'd be
called to the front and handed a sheet of lyrics. Following a brief
huddle by the band members, the song would begin, and the vocalist would get to experience the sensation of being a rock star—
albeit a rock star playing a second-tier club with no cover charge.
Each time I volunteered at Arlene's, I'd inevitably repeat some
variation of the above inner monologue, one that was entirely hy-
perbolic. In reality, the bar's official capacity was around seventy
people, and while there were some alluring rocker girls, there were
also large pockets of dudes—the type of dudes who liked to hang
out by the beer taps and talk about rare Stooges bootlegs.

   As for that bassist, he wasn't actually scowling at me; he was
simply grimacing under the strain of trying to drink, smoke, and
play guitar all at once. Though the Original Punk Rock/Heavy
Metal Karaoke Band didn't have to worry about such "real band"
tasks as writing songs or coddling an egomaniacal lead singer, the

gig presented the band members with a series of unique challenges: Over the next few years, they'd have to deal with botched gigs, ill-advised flings, grumpy-fan revolts, and one very public firing. And they'd also be forced to play "Anarchy in the U.K." more times than the Sex Pistols ever did. I really couldn't blame any of them for wanting to drink on the job.

The history of the Arlene's band begins in Los Angeles, where the first Punk Karaoke Band formed in 1996. With a rotating lineup that included former members of Bad Religion and Social Distortion, the L.A. Punk Karaoke Band played clubs around California, eventually touring nationwide with the 1998 Warped Tour. In early 1999, a New York City record-label owner named Lael Sturm caught one of the group's shows at a Hollywood club, and upon returning home, he mentioned the live-band concept to Rob Kemp, a bassist and writer for *Time Out New York* magazine. Kemp didn't have a full-time band, but he'd been practicing with Devin Emke, a guitarist he'd known since childhood, and David Richman, a former drummer for '90s alt-rock group Letters to Cleo. Kemp offered the trio's services, and Sturm used a connection at Arlene's to secure the band a one-off gig. The date was set for Monday, April 20—giving the musicians only two months to rehearse nearly twenty-five songs.

"I remember not going to work that day, because I was so fucking freaked about playing," Kemp tells me seven years later, drinking a beer on a Sunday afternoon in Brooklyn. He has glasses and a short haircut with rolls of curls, and even though we've known each other socially for a few years, his fixed stare is just as unreadable as it was when I met him nearly a decade ago. The first Punk Rock Karaoke Band gig drew about fifty people, many of them friends or coworkers whom the group members had wrangled into attending. This qualified as a decent Monday-night turnout, especially in a neighborhood that had yet to be commodified by boutique stores and upscale grilled-cheese restaurants. So the club's booker gave the band a semi-regular 10 P.M. slot. "We didn't think it would be as popular as it was," Kemp says. "But once the word is out that there's this thing where *anybody* can get on stage, people are going to show up."

Because the live-band karaoke format was so unknown, those who did make it to the band's early shows sometimes had to be coaxed on stage. At the very first Arlene's gig that Mike and I attended in the summer of 1999, the band's emcee—a cranky, wiry Brit named Owen Comaskey—was forced to perform some of the songs himself, even though the club was full of potential volunteers. In those early days, Kemp feared there'd come a time when *nobody* in the audience wanted to sing. "Then what are we gonna do?" he remembers worrying. "No one wants to see us play the song by ourselves."

By the end of the summer, though, an encouraging preshow ritual was taking place around 9:45 each Monday night. That's when a group of cordial but visibly anxious fans amassed by the front of the stage to wait for the sign-up sheet to be passed into the crowd, where it was lobbed around like a beach ball. The competition for the list could be tense, as the band rarely repeated songs during the night; if you didn't call dibs on the Clash in time, you'd have to try again the next week.

Once the list had made its way through the audience, Comaskey—who was not only the show's emcee but also the club's booker—would take to the mic, full of cackle and bark. A former punk who'd lived in Birmingham during the late '70s, Comaskey stood at the front of Arlene's while bathed in red spotlights and stray cigarette smoke, which made him look a bit like a mad English devil. It was mostly shtick, of course, but I still found him slightly

intimidating, so I tried to keep my Punk Rock Karaoke performances as brief as possible. This is why I usually chose to sing the
Misfits' "Attitude," as it's only a minute and a half long, made up of
brief couplets like "Inside your feeble brain/there's probably a
whore." It was a good song for someone who wanted to get on and
off the stage quickly, though not so much for someone hoping to
meet girls. When I was finished, I'd swiftly negotiate my way to the
back of the room, where I'd drink a beer, accept a few cursory
plaudits, and wait for the regulars to go on.

Unlike many public karaoke bars—where the song choices can
be predictable, and the performances too self-consciously
showy—Arlene's was ideal for spectators, as it tended to attract
part-time extroverts. Many of the people who showed up had office jobs, and they were looking for a place where they could
scream and flail without judgment. One early attendee was Aaron
Jaffe, an editor at the *Wall Street Journal* who looked a bit like a
long-haired Mick Jones (from the Clash, not Foreigner). He went
to his first Arlene's show in November 1999, and though the club
was almost empty that night, Jaffe was still nervous. "I picked 'No
Fun' by the Stooges, because that seemed easy," he tells me. "I
joked to the band, 'You know, if I really want to do it right, I guess
I have to take my shirt off.' And believe me, nobody needs to see
me with my shirt off."

Jaffe's performances were memorably spastic—when describing
them, he uses "trainwreck" as a verb—and he soon became a favorite among the show's attendees. "People I didn't know would
come up to me and say, 'Did you go yet? We came to see you,'" he
says. "Even if it was bullshit, hell, people know who I am, and what
I do up there."

Another punk-band perennial was John McDonough, a jazz-
trumpet player who was hard to miss at the early shows, as he

usually wore a porkpie hat and glasses while screaming Bad Brains lyrics. McDonough had played with several jazz combos and marching bands, yet he had never worked up the courage to sing, as he feared his voice would sound unpolished and raw. With punk rock, this was actually an asset, so he researched the band's setlist and then prepared for his debut by practicing the Damned's "New Rose" at home. "The first few times I went up there, I was thinking, 'Oh my God, what are they gonna think of me when I butcher this song?'" he says. "After a while, I got less concerned about the crowd reaction. It was very cathartic. I got a lot of my aggressions out." McDonough was in his early thirties when he began frequenting Arlene's, and he'd missed out on the punk scene of the late '70s. This was his chance to catch up. "I'd never gone to punk shows as a kid," he says. "I never moshed. I never stage-dove. Karaoke was the first time I actually did that. I felt a little self-conscious doing it, but it was still great."

On his second night at Arlene's, McDonough met Jaffe, and the two quickly became friends. Soon enough, everyone in the front-stage huddle knew each other's names, and often they shared the same rock and roll obsessions. If there was one common trait among all the early punk-metal devotees, Jaffe says, it was that they were all music geeks. And music geeks are not exactly renowned for their social-situation ease. "A lot of people saw this as an outlet to come out of their shell," he says. "Some of them are shy, and have a hard time approaching people. But you put 'em on stage, and there's something coming out of them." •

To sing at Arlene's was to be initiated into a gang, albeit a decidedly nonthreatening one: New recruits weren't hazed with violence, but with copious amounts of Captain Beefheart trivia. After a worthy performance, the anonymous faces in the audience would often give newcomers an approving nod, or even better, a free round. "You'd go there every week, not just for the chance to go on stage, but because you were seeing the same people every week," Jaffe says. "And it quickly became a tight circle of people. You knew if you walked in there on a Monday night: instant friends."

Which is not to say that performing with the band wasn't intimidating. The stage at Arlene's was only a few feet from the floor, but when you took that step up, the change in altitude put hornets in your head and pins in your stomach—especially when you saw all the people clinging to the front of the stage, waiting to be entertained. Such attention, of course, is one of the reasons karaoke became so popular to begin with. But live-band karaoke perhaps best replicates the experience of being a professional singer, with no on-screen vocals to guide you along, and no predictable backing tracks. Instead, you're given a sheet of paper with some lyrics, and before you even know what you've gotten into, the drummer is counting off the song. "For those three minutes, you are up *there*, and all those people are down *there*," Kemp says. "You are the fucking emphasis."

In November 1999, the Arlene's band played its first-ever all-metal show. I was there that night, and I remember it for two reasons:

1. The guest emcee for the evening was George Tabb, an infamously caustic *New York Press* columnist who was hired, Kemp says, because he was "good at running his mouth." Tabb began the show by asking a woman in the audience if her breasts were real, prompting the woman's friend—an imposing blonde wearing a bikini and a sharp

ring on her finger—to walk on stage, scream in Tabb's
face, and sock him in the jaw. Tabb then introduced
Quiet Riot's "Bang Your Head," which he sang with blood
trickling from his mouth.

2. From that night on, the Arlene's band would have little
   difficulty getting people on stage.

Introducing metal was a controversial move among the band's
punk-karaoke loyalists. Some objected to the music for purely aesthetic reasons, while others complained that a song like the Misfits' "Attitude" would lose its antiestablishment power if it was
played alongside Iron Maiden's "Run to the Hills." "It's absurd that
anybody would be ideological or political about the difference between punk rock and heavy metal," says Kemp. "But people were.
And people would get mad that we were playing heavy metal music. It was like 1982 again. People would come up to me and say, 'I
can't believe you guys are doing that. Iron Maiden is *against* the
Misfits.'"

To appease both audiences, the band initially kept punk and
metal separate, relegating AC/DC and its ilk to one night a month.
But the '77-era purists were soon outnumbered by the '80s nostal-
gists, and at the time, hair-metal was in the midst of cultural reap-
praisal: A circa–*Appetite for Destruction* picture of Axl Rose had
just appeared on the cover of *Spin,* and VH1's high-rated *Behind
the Music* had somehow managed to make even Ratt's backstory
seem compelling. So the members of the Punk Rock Karaoke
Band combined the two setlists, rechristening themselves the
Original Punk Rock/Heavy Metal Karaoke Band. The merger was
not without its critics, including Comaskey, who took breaks from
his emcee duties to launch into on-stage diatribes about the awful-
ness of Guns N' Roses (to this day, he still regards *Appetite* as the

worst album ever made). Within a few weeks, though, the complaints died down, and the accessibility of Poison and Twisted Sister songs attracted a larger, far more egalitarian crowd, one that included not just music geeks, but also inquisitive yuppies and ex-jocks. The shows at Arlene's became kinetic and untamed, and ironically, it was only with the inclusion of heavy metal that the gigs took on a truly punk-rock feel.

Once the songlist expanded, I found myself venturing to Arlene's more frequently, usually with Mike or Kevin, and I even kept a spare Van Halen T-shirt in my work cubicle, just in case there was an unexpected Monday-night outing. We'd show up early, watch the last few songs from whatever middling local band had secured the opening slot, and then join the crowd for the 9:45 P.M. rush. With so many new metal songs, the competition to get on the list intensified, and I spent months trying to claim Def Leppard's "Photograph," which always seemed to be taken by the time I got to the list. So I'd pick something by Zeppelin or Van Halen, and bide my hours scoping out the new regulars. Many of the heavy-metal singers seemed more theatrical than their punk-rock counterparts—not to mention louder. Cindy Ball, a writer and costume designer, remembers going to her first Arlene's show in the spring of 2001, more than a year after metal karaoke was introduced. "The first thing that happened was that this tiny, cute-as-a-button Asian woman gets on stage," Ball remembers. "She seems really nervous. I'm not really sure what to expect. Then she belts out Motörhead with this voice that came from hell. I was like, 'This is perfect. This is *exactly* where I need to be.'"

One of the more popular metal-era regulars was a young Brooklynite whom everyone knew as Paulie Z. He'd first come to Arlene's on a date in 2000, when he performed Kiss's "Detroit Rock City" only to be disappointed by the band's sloppy rendition.

Before the end of the night, however, the group put out a request to see if anyone wanted to perform Deep Purple's "Highway Star," and Z once again volunteered. "I tore the house down on that one," he says. "I was hooked. How can you not be?" When Z was finished, someone on stage asked him his name. "Nobody ever called me Paulie, but I didn't want to use my whole name. So I said 'Paulie Z,' and this was where this persona started."

The Paulie Z "persona" was that of a Brooklyn-proud hard rocker, kind of like Vinnie Barbarino hosting *Headbanger's Ball*. Whereas many of the singers let their energy out in three-minute spurts before retreating to the bar, Paulie and his brother, David Z, seemed to keep performing even when they weren't on stage, and could often be seen at the very front of the crowd, pumping their fists in encouragement. The Z Brothers became fixtures at Arlene's: They formed a Kiss tribute act, which played its very first gig opening up for the Original Punk Rock/Heavy Metal Karaoke Band. Paulie and David even hosted a special evening of "Millennium Karaoke," during which they performed songs by Stone Temple Pilots, Nirvana, and Pearl Jam (Kemp, in a rare verbal turn at the mic, performed a Creed song). "We were very good friends with the band," Paulie Z says. "They came to my freakin' house for my birthday party."

By the fall of 2001, the Arlene's karaoke band had earned a modest but adamant following as well as write-ups in the *New York Times* and *MOJO* magazine. A local filmmaker named Sonny Aronson had put together a documentary on the band, and there were celebrity guests, including Ryan Adams, Melissa Auf Der Mar from Smashing Pumpkins, and Jimmy Fallon and Horatio Sanz from *Saturday Night Live*. I once looked into the crowd while singing and saw *Party of Five*'s Scott Wolf, who was making out with a girl, and therefore missing out on my lively version of Van Halen's "Panama."

The band began booking private gigs around the city, but the members remained loyal to Arlene's, where they were earning about $50 each on Monday nights from the club, plus audience tips. In addition to the money, the gig provided some incalculable fringe benefits: Though guitarist Emke had gotten married just a few weeks before the band's first show, Kemp and drummer Richman were single for long stretches of the group's heyday at Arlene's. "That's a motivation to make music that you can never truly discount," Kemp says. "When you're up there, and you have certain kinds of rock 'n' roll moves, there will be women." Adds Richman: "When I broke up with the girlfriend and became single, every woman I dated, I'd met on the gig."

Because the crowd was hopped up on a mix of booze, adrenaline, and Judas Priest songs, it's not surprising that the club became a reliable pick-up spot, for both the band and the audience. "You see the soul of a person when they're singing," says Vincent Guagenti, a film-school teacher who watched many of his friends pair off together after a show. "If someone you're interested in gets up there and has the balls, it makes that somebody much more attractive. That person screaming at you on the microphone is the same person who's going to be screaming at you in bed."

The downside to these post-show flings was that many of them didn't last longer than a few days (or hours), which made for some uneasy Monday-night reunions. "There were times that I made a decision that wasn't terribly good, and then that woman always knew where I was," says Kemp. "That was sort of awkward— 'Man, I fucked that girl, and I kind of wished that I didn't, and now she's up here singing Aerosmith and making eyes at me. This is weird.'" Adds Cindy Ball: "There were a couple of breakups. And I said, 'You know what? If you want to keep coming to karaoke, then you've got to choke it down. You've gotta clap when your ex-paramour performs. You can't be chased away.'"

The majority of the off-stage fraternizing, though, was relatively chaste. Some of the regulars at Arlene's formed bands, while others went to movies and concerts together; Jaffe even served as the officiator at Guagenti's wedding. For many of the live-band faithful, the shows became the hub of their social life, and Monday nights turned into their Friday nights. "More than one person has said that when they went to Arlene's, they felt like they had come home," Kemp says.

In 2001, after two years of building up a loyal following, the band members felt confident enough to once again change the musical direction of the karaoke shows, at least temporarily. The one-night-only "Arena-rock karaoke" was to focus on late-'70s and early-'80s acts like Styx, Foreigner, and Asia. And while there were some conscientious objectors within the audience—to many people, Journey is even more godless than Iron Maiden—such hackles were pretty much ignored. The band members learned more than forty songs, and they hyped the show for months from the stage. But they almost lost the gig altogether when Kemp left his bass guitar in the back of a cab. He never recovered it, but luckily he had an old Rickenbacker stored in his closet. He fixed it up just days before the concert. The guitar didn't sound that great, but at least it would be ready by the night of the show: September 10, 2001.

⌒

Like many people who use popular-cultural events to mark their lives, I can walk into a video store or listen to the radio and pinpoint the *exact* date on which a movie or album came out. This is not an especially unique or impressive skill; in fact, it's rather sad, and I have no shortage of guilt over the fact that I can recall *Bat-*

man's opening date (June 23, 1989) off the top of my head, and yet have only a vague memory of when the Marshall Plan was enacted (maybe 1971?). But it *does* affect the way I think about 9/11. Whenever I happen upon some cultural work from the past decade or so, especially anything released between 2000–2002, my mind automatically files it as pre-9/11 or post-9/11, and that position completely screws with my critical judgment: Everything from the spring and summer of 2001 makes me feel wistful, because, in retrospect, it was consumed during a time when I didn't have much to worry about. But any movie, book, TV show, or album that I absorbed the fall of 2001 to the spring of 2002 is underscored with sadness. By this criterion, *A Beautiful Mind* is an absolute hoot, while Mariah Carey's *Glitter* is the most depressing film ever released.

All of which goes to say: I remember the arena-rock karaoke show as being thoroughly awesome. But then again, I could be wrong.

What I do know was that competition for the sign-up sheet that night was especially fierce. Mike and I showed up early, but so had everyone else, and by the time the list got to us, there were so many occupied slots that we had no choice but to sign up for Loverboy's "Workin' for the Weekend" as a duo. As we stood by the front of the bar, waiting for the show to begin, a formidable-looking keyboard was hauled out, one that appeared to take up almost half the stage. The punk-metal trio had gone to the trouble of hiring a back-up keyboardist, a traditional benchmark of rock-star hubris, and proof that the band members were treating the arena-rock show with all due pomposity. Suddenly, the show began to feel like a real concert.

The performers that night were a mix of regulars old and new. Paulie Z opened the show, performing Boston's seven-minute-long "Foreplay/Long Time," thus justifying the inclusion of that keyboard (which would later be used for Styx's equally protracted "Come Sail Away"). Guagenti had shown up, too, bringing along a group of U.S. Marines he'd met earlier in the day at a biker bar. When the soldiers asked him where they could meet women in the city, he piled them into his truck and brought them to Arlene's. Once in the club, Guagenti remembers, "It was like *Popeye*. One guy was like, 'I can't sing.' So I said, 'If it was up to you to defend your country by singing "Paradise City," would you do it?' He said, 'Yes, I would!' I got him all psyched up, so we got his ass on stage."

After an hour or so, Mike and I got our shot at "Workin' for the Weekend," trading off verses with ease and moving up and down the stage with semi-choreographed struts, as if those years at Village Karaoke had all been inadvertent practice for tonight. This was going to be our last karaoke together for the next few months: Mike was scheduled to move to Vienna, Austria, that week for a new job, and he had an as-yet-undetermined return date. So we celebrated long after our performance was over, drinking until 3 A.M., at which point I went back to Brooklyn, and Mike went for a walk around Manhattan with our friend Walter. Upon reaching 14th Street and 7th Avenue, they heard a homeless man singing Hall & Oates' "Maneater," and together, the three of them chanted "Woah-ohh, here she comes" in the predawn.

Early the next morning, I went to the *Entertainment Weekly* offices, turned on the news, and quickly walked down to Mike's apartment in Manhattan, where we watched the TV for hours on end. Mike's trip was delayed for a while, but the Original Punk Rock/Heavy Metal Karaoke Band returned to Arlene's the very next week, though I never saw them play there again. This was partly because Mike wound up being in Vienna for nearly two years, and his absence would have made it a lot less fun to hang around the front of the stage jostling for the sign-up sheet. But mostly, I didn't go back to Arlene's because I didn't want to create any new memories—not of the bar, not of the band, and not of the time spent with them both. Instead, I wanted to preserve that night the way I remember it now: one last oblivious bop around the city, right before the start of an unwelcome new timeline.

The Original Punk/Rock Heavy Metal Band continued playing Arlene's for the next three years, drawing a reliable Monday-night crowd. During that time, the group had little interaction with the club's owners, usually negotiating for raises with the help of Comaskey, the club's booker. But in the summer of 2004, the relationship between the band members and management began to sour. Comaskey, who'd become preoccupied with developing a separate MTV show, was let go that summer, and though he briefly stayed on as the group's emcee, the band members now had to deal with management on their own. The Original Punk Rock/Heavy Metal shows had been part of the club's line-up for more than five years, and Kemp, Emke, and Richman were now earning $100 each per show, plus anywhere from $20 to $50 each in tips. With Emke expecting a baby, Kemp went to the owners and asked for $200 a night (an amount he now admits was "fucking crazy"). He also negotiated for the time slot to be moved up an hour to 9 P.M., so that Emke could get home earlier.

Almost immediately, Kemp realized he'd made a mistake. Because many of the regulars still showed up at 10 P.M., the first hour of those Monday nights soon became sluggish, a problem for both the band and the bar. After only a few weeks, the three band members went to Arlene's management and said they were willing to move the time back and reduce their fee. Yet they could sense they'd fallen out of favor with the club. On November 3, 2004, shortly after arriving in Florida for a vacation, Kemp received an urgent phone call from Richman, who told him the band had just been fired. According to Richman, the club's management had secretly recruited and trained a new group of musicians to take the band's place, a charge that a club representative firmly denies.

Kemp spent his time in Florida on the phone with his bandmates and friends, and the group's plight earned a mention in the *New York Post*'s infamous "Page Six" section, under the headline "BAND'S FIRING ROCKS HOT CLUB." A few weeks later, on the same night that the new band was scheduled to make its debut at Arlene's, Kemp, Emke, and Richman gathered with some of their fans in a bar just down the street. During the course of the evening, some of the revelers got loaded enough to head over to Arlene's and check out their replacements. "Dave described it as watching another guy fuck your girlfriend," says Emke. "Which I guess was a pretty good description."

In January 2005, Kemp, Emke, and Richman were offered a residency at Continental, a club near Manhattan's once-skeevy St. Marks Place. Though the Continental was just a quick cab ride from Arlene's, the two clubs may as well have been in different cities: In the five years since the band had started playing at Arlene's, the Lower East Side had expanded to include more restaurants and bars, drawing moneyed hipsters and cachet-seeking tourists alike. St. Marks, however, had become a sort of faux-punk ghetto, a place to buy fart-joke T-shirts or bongs. Some of the longtime followers weren't willing to make the commute, including the Z Brothers, whose new band, Z02, was now playing regular gigs at Arlene's. The Original Punk Rock/Heavy Metal Karaoke Band couldn't secure a following at Continental and began to drift from one club to the next, unable to replicate the fan base it enjoyed in its heyday. The Continental gig, says Emke, "was certainly the beginning of the decline for us."

On a Wednesday night in early 2007, I went to my first proper Original Punk Rock/Heavy Metal Karaoke Band concert in more than three years. The band had played Mike's thirtieth birthday party a few months earlier, and for the occasion the members had learned Body Count's 1989 repetitive thrash anthem "Body Count's in the House." While Mike and I were happy to chant the song's titular chorus over and over again—and, for once, not just to each other—I'm fairly certain the band has had little use for it since.

The show was at Southpaw, a five-year-old club in the Park Slope neighborhood of Brooklyn. A few days before the gig, Kemp had expressed concern about the neighborhood's demographics: Southpaw's line-up generally consisted of indie-rock and hip-hop shows, plus something called Baby Loves Disco, a toddler dance party that's indicative of the area's young-parent demographic. Indeed, when the band started to play at 9:30 P.M., there were only about thirty people in the audience, many of whom I recognized from Arlene's. Guagenti was one of the first performers, singing Sweet's "Ballroom Blitz." He later told me he'd been trying to convince the band members to learn the song for five years.

On stage, Kemp, Emke, and Richman all looked much like they did in 1999, still wearing T-shirts and jeans, still playing with precision and minimal fussiness. But while Kemp kept a can of Tecate on top of his bass amp, it was his only drink for the first two hours. And though the crowd members were hardly sedate, many of them seemed perfectly content standing in one place and mildly banging their heads. At one point, a mosh pit broke out, but it was brief and a bit forced.

The band's songbook had expanded to about 250 songs, including Duran Duran's "Hungry Like the Wolf" and Kelly Clarkson's "Since U Been Gone." Still, when it was my turn, I selected Led Zeppelin's "Immigrant Song," an old standby that I dedicated, unfunnily, to Lou Dobbs. I hopped up and down on all the wrong beats, and I felt surprisingly nervous—maybe because I couldn't hear my *aughhh-a-AHHHHHHH . . . ahhh!* in the monitor, or maybe out of sheer nostalgia.

The Southpaw gig was booked just as the band's career appeared to be winding down. Emke and Richman were both married, and their recent pursuits had been more lucrative than the occasional stint playing "Sweet Child O' Mine" (Emke is now an audio engineer for *Saturday Night Live,* while Richman works as a production director at Razor & Tie records). "At this point, there's nothing that is inspiring me to do this," Richman had told me a few days before the show. "The timeline is not much longer."

In the months after the Southpaw show, I kept waiting for an announcement that the band had broken up. Instead, I received constant e-mails about new live dates. Some of these shows went spectacularly unwell, drawing only two or three people. But in October 2007, there was a last-minute gig opening for a Kid Rock record-release party in New York City, and just before Christmas, the band performed at a holiday party for a Long Island auto dealership (the show lasted only thirty minutes, and it consisted mostly of inebriated employees demanding Jay-Z songs, but it remained the biggest payday of the band's career). By the summer of 2008, the Original Punk Rock/Heavy Metal Karaoke Band had secured a twice-monthly booking at Rehab, a Lower East Side club just a few blocks away from the club that had exiled them years before. "There's a community of people that's risen around us," Kemp says. "It can get a little insular, and it can get a little entitled, and it can be a little impenetrable for new people. But we do have this solid base that we can depend on."

At Southpaw, I'd asked Jaffe, perhaps the band's longest-running fan, how much longer he could keep turning up for punk-metal karaoke. He'd just had his first kid and was about to turn forty, but he waved the question away. "I never get the sense of, 'Oh, now it's time to grow up,' you know?" he told me. "The whole point of everything is not to grow up." Not long afterward, he was on the stage, singing the Dead Kennedys' "Kill the Poor," and throwing his long black hair around so madly that it almost obscured his grin.

CHAPTER 4

Don't Disturb This Groove

I KEEP TWO LISTS IN MY HEAD WHENEVER I GO TO A NEW KARAOKE VENUE. THE FIRST COLLECTS THE SONGS I'VE ALWAYS WANTED TO SING, but have never been able to find. There are about fifty or so titles on this list at any given time, including:

- Prince, "I Could Never Take the Place of Your Man"
- Genesis, "Illegal Alien"
- Joe Walsh, "In the City"
- Nick Lowe, "So It Goes"
- The System, "Don't Disturb This Groove"
- The Rubinoos, "I Never Thought It Would Happen"
- Anything ever written by Superchunk

This list used to be much longer, but now that it's possible to squeeze thousands of karaoke tracks into a hard drive, I don't have to search as diligently as I did nearly ten years ago. Back then, it could take months for new songs to materialize at Village Karaoke, which they did in unexpected, unannounced bursts. Our only other option was to purchase the karaoke tracks ourselves, as a few dealers offered expensive custom-made discs (for Mike's twenty-fourth birthday, I bought him a Jefferson Starship compilation that set me back $70, making it only slightly less expensive than hiring the actual members of Jefferson Starship). So we waited patiently for the songbooks to be updated, and when a slew of '90s grunge tracks showed up one night at Sing Sing on the Lower East Side, Mike and I whooped like drought-averting farmers.

Even after all these years, though, there remain several glaring omissions on my wish list, which I suspect will only grow longer and stranger as I get older. Every day, I'm consumed with half a dozen or so new songs, and after they've played in my head for a while, they start banging the roof of my brain with an upturned hockey stick, demanding to be let out somehow. Sometimes this is an annoyance, such as when that banging is done by "Mambo No. 5." But usually, I'm more than happy to turn them loose, because I want to share them with others. The only problem is that, nowadays, songs have nowhere to go.

I realize this sounds strange, considering that we're living at a time when music is so pervasive in our culture, and when it can easily be shared, gifted, beamed, embedded, and siphoned. But in the past thirty years, the act of *consuming* music has become more insular. One major reason for this is the 1979 introduction of the Walkman, which made it possible to listen to an album or the radio without bothering anyone else. Yet early Walkmans were expensive, and were considered so much of a nuisance that many schools and workplaces banned them altogether. It wasn't until the introduction of the iPod—which started out as a luxury item, and which now sells for less than $150—that *everyone* suddenly had a portable listening device, which they'd wear to the office, school, or the gym, always stuck in their own private world. These worlds are open to others at times, and I'm always charmed when I see school kids splitting their iPod headphones on the subway, so that they can both listen to the same song (I'm less enamored when those same kids' cell phones start up with a crackly version of Soulja Boy Slim's "Crank Dat"). But oftentimes, songs today remain pent up, stuck behind earbuds. Which is why, when I'm really stuck on a song and need to let it out, I rent a private karaoke room.

Getting a k-box for a few hours is akin to starting up a radio station with your friends—all your favorite hits, plus a few bad comedy sketches. It's where good songs are revered and shared, and where individual musical quirks are laid bare. At karaoke, you learn which of your friends secretly loves Andrew Lloyd Webber or Hanson, and they get to share these songs with you in person. You can't get that sort of immediacy with file-sharing—or with mixtapes, as much as I miss them. With the exception of live music itself, karaoke may be the most direct form of music appreciation that exists, which is why I hope that all those songs wind up on karaoke someday. I've never been able to pay them their proper due, and until I do, they'll still be lodged in my brain, kicking around.

That's why I also keep my second karaoke songlist, this one compiling the tracks that I can always find, and which I've yet to grow tired of, despite the fact that I always sing them. I'm not claiming that I can perform these with any discernable skill, but at least I know all of the words:

- Bobby Brown, "On Our Own"
- Mike + the Mechanics, "All I Need Is a Miracle"
- Dan Hartman, "I Can Dream about You"
- Elton John, "I Guess That's Why They Call It the Blues"

- Looking Glass, "Brandy (You're a Fine Girl)"
- Stevie Nicks, "Stand Back"

If you were to combine both lists, you'd have a pretty good overview of the songs I tend to favor at karaoke. There are some overdramatic ballads, a few bright power-pop numbers, and lots of '80s blue-eyed soul. You'd also have a list that some music fans and critics would no doubt find revolting, as the majority of these songs are hardly considered classics. Prince and Nick Lowe are all but untouchable, and Superchunk—a long-running guitar-rock outfit from Chapel Hill, North Carolina—is one of only a handful of bands that have never written a truly bad song. But a group like the System is in many ways indefensible: The duo's "Don't Disturb This Groove" may be a prodigious work of techno-funk, but the song's smooth-talking vocals are so corny that it makes me think of two guys wearing silk bathrobes in the studio.

And yet, while I wouldn't necessarily put these songs on a personal Top 10 list, I'd eagerly sing them in public. If karaoke is indeed a form of music appreciation, then I've come to realize that I mostly appreciate crap. My already dodgy musical tastes are completely negated in a karaoke room. When I actually perform a song, its merits are not measured aesthetically, but pragmatically: Does this song take too long to the chorus? Have I forgotten how the intro goes? Will it be performed five more times tonight? If I wimp out before the bridge, will I be disturbing any grooves? More often than not, karaoke rewards songs that appeal to our base desires, not our intellect. It is music's great context-converter, and no two songs demonstrate this better than Bob Dylan's "Like a Rolling Stone" and Bobby Brown's "On Our Own."

In 2004, *Rolling Stone* magazine named "Like a Rolling Stone" the greatest song of all time. There was a period in my life when I used to get worked up over such lists, but the final-word authority that these sorts of decrees held in the '80s and '90s has been eroded by the Internet, where an updated Greatest Shit Ever index is published each time a new *Saw* sequel comes out. No one publication or person carries enough weight (or demands a large enough audience) to lend these lists any credibility.

The commendation of "Like a Rolling Stone" was not entirely surprising: At some point in the past thirty years, the country's music critics convened a star chamber to decide that Dylan's song is, indeed, the greatest of all time. Anyone who tries to oppose that stance will be out-nayed and over-harumphed by the baby boomers who use "Stone" to remind us how revolutionary they were in the '60s (curiously, these same boomers tend to downplay any song that emphasizes how debauched they became in the '80s, when they traded free-love ideology for junk bonds, cocaine, and divorce lawyers; if they did, I imagine Glenn Frey would be just as lionized as Bob Dylan). I resent the '60s generations' constant pasturbation, which in recent years has started to sound like a fear-of-death rattle, and yet I enjoy "Like a Rolling Stone." I may not enjoy it as much as other Dylan numbers like "Lay Lady Lay" or "Tangled Up in Blue," but I do think the song's constant acclaim is deserved. I just think it sounds terrible at karaoke.

Thankfully, it doesn't get picked too often. But when it does, the results are excruciating: six minutes of Dylan's rise-and-fall verses, undertaken by someone who really only remembers the chorus. There's a look of surprise on the singer's face, then gradual panic, then loss, and then resigned acceptance. The performer doesn't enjoy it, and neither does the crowd. "Stone" sounds perfectly fine when it's on the radio, but at karaoke, it's a drag. Over the years I've developed my own set of criteria for determining whether a given song will make a good karaoke performance, and "Like a Rolling Stone" lacks all three:

1. Mystery

On the rare occasions that I sing at a crowded karaoke bar—as opposed to the more expensive, yet less formidable k-box room—I calm myself by thinking that, no matter what goes down, only half of the people in attendance are actually paying attention to me. This works for the first thirty seconds or so, until I suddenly invert that theory and realize that, if my calculations are correct, then the other half is *definitely* paying attention. What's worse, they're waiting for their turn to sing, and to them I'm nothing but a time-consuming obstacle. These are the people I need to entertain, and although I don't need to sing especially well to do so, I have to keep them from getting impatient, lest they turn on me completely and pelt me with ashtrays and napkins. And nothing will test an audience's patience more than a song they've already heard a few thousand times already—a song that's so worn out that it's absolutely impossible to listen to in a new way.

"Like a Rolling Stone" is such a song. It belongs in a rarefied musical stratum, one made entirely of tunes that I never need to hear at karaoke ever again: "My Way," "Let It Be," "(I Can't Get No) Satisfaction." These are the songs with absolutely no mystery left—nothing to discover. If I have to watch people sing for three hours, I want to be surprised at least a few times, whether it's by individual song choices or by some wildly unprecedented interpretation. I'd rather hear a way-off-key but enthusiastic version of a song I've never heard before—or that I've dismissed in the past—than a spot-on version of "Like a Rolling Stone." As elitist as it sounds, I'll politely ignore the guy singing "Stone" at the karaoke bar, praying that the next performer is a crazy Gulf War vet who dresses as a train conductor and scats all the words to some Peabo Bryson song that I didn't even know about. It's not an ideal situation, but at least I'll learn something.[1]

Yet while most people are overly familiar with Dylan's tune, Bobby Brown's "On Our Own" has the rare distinction of being a Top 10 hit that many people have completely forgotten about. It was one of two songs that Brown contributed to the soundtrack for *Ghostbusters II* in 1989, and though I don't remember the name of the first one, I imagine it was something like "Girl (Ya Spook Me)." Unlike most songs that get bundled into such cash-in collections, "Own" incorporated specific characters and scenes from the movie into its lyrics, and woefully so: There are multiple references to slime, and an entire rap that culminates with a dig at Vigo, the film's villainous physical manifestation of New York City's negative energy. To this day, I don't know if Brown was inspired to write these couplets after an early screening, or if he just took an old track, tried to rhyme the words "Vigo" and "evil," and then took the money and used it to go to Atlantic City and buy some new leather bicycle shorts.

"On Our Own" never hit No. 1 on the Billboard Hot 100; instead, it was stalled at No. 2, thwarted by Prince's "Batdance."

---

1. I don't mean to imply that there are no classic-rock songs that will work as karaoke songs. It's just that so many hits of the '60s and '70s have been performed, analyzed, satirized, and ultimately repurposed for so long that their ubiquity has left them powerless. The hits from that era that I still find enjoyable to sing are the ones that have endured as actual songs, rather than being turned into cultural emblems: the Stones' "Beast of Burden," the Who's "I Can See for Miles," and Led Zeppelin's "Out on the Tiles," for example.

Neither song gets much radio play anymore, but at least Prince could ride the *Batman* mania for a few more sequels. "Own," however, had a built-in expiration date, and by the summer of 1990, at which time *Ghostbusters II* was already on video, America had moved on to Snap!'s "The Power." Suddenly, Brown's lyrics about proton packs seemed a lot less urgent.

But for anyone who heard the song when it came out, "On Our Own" is impossible to truly forget, and if I were to recite the song's key couplet ("too hot to handle/too cold to hold"), pieces of the song would begin to fall in place: You might be able to vaguely recall its melody, or its repeated utterances of "ya-ya ya-know-it." Yet there would still be some nagging gaps in your memory, and these could all be satisfied at karaoke, where a twenty-year-old song like "On Our Own" might actually sound new again.

For the most part, those two lists at the beginning of the chapter are made up of second-tier songs—they're the tracks that experienced massive radio success, yet never made it to the top of the Billboard chart. The public never had a chance to become tired of "On Our Own," nor with a song like Elton John's "I Guess That's Why They Call It the Blues," which reached No. 4 on the Billboard singles chart. Compare it to "Can You Feel the Love Tonight?" or "Candle in the Wind"—songs that are so culturally widespread, they all but disappear into the background—and you can see why "Blues" is a far more desirable karaoke number: Much like "On Our Own," the song was popular, but never pervasive, and that allows it to remain relatively fresh in listeners' minds.

2. Diversity

In terms of vocals, not much happens in "Like a Rolling Stone." There are the winding "once upon a time" verses, and the *feel-eel*s choruses, and while I don't doubt that they're initially exciting to perform, the song rarely changes. There's no bridge, just harmonica breakdowns, and the tempo never shifts: It keeps going at the same pace until it leaves you exhausted on stage, beaten down by repetition.

"On Our Own," by contrast, is vocally nimble. It consists of three sections, each one requiring a different approach: the half-sung, half-spoken verses; the straightforward soul-vocal chorus; and a frenetically delivered mid-song rap. The music itself is unobtrusive—just a few drum-machine beats and some afterthought piano. It was written during the height of the New Jack Swing era, a time in the late '80s and early '90s when R&B artists were trying to appease soul-Glo loverboys, *Club MTV* dancers, and hip-hop fans who wanted to glower and dance at the same time. As a result, "On Our Own" tries to be everything to everyone in just four and a half minutes.

That overcooked arrangement, though, helps make "Own" an immensely pleasurable karaoke experience. The song changes every thirty seconds or so, and because it's constantly in motion, neither the singer nor the audience grows weary of it. There's a reason why "Bohemian Rhapsody" is one of the most popular karaoke selections in the world: It's constantly changing. If a singer gets bored with the opening, he or she can wait for the operatic bridge or the arena-rock diatribe at the end. "Rhapsody" may be just as overexposed as "Like a Rolling Stone," but because it offers so many different parts, so many possible interpretations, it's an exception to that first rule.

As a perhaps unintentional benefit, "On Our Own" allows those of us without flow to rap freely and without self-consciousness. Even our honkiest Americans could do a half-decent impression of Bobby Brown, who delivers the "too hot to handle/too cold to hold" line with all the dexterity and concern of a guy trying to order a sandwich. If he can't be bothered to rap effectively on his own song, why should we?

3. Absurdity

I have nothing but disdain for overly ironic karaoke performances, in which the singers eye-roll their way through a song, making sure *we* know that *they* know that the whole contemptible experience is beneath them. These people want it both ways—flaunting their supposed love of music while simultaneously mocking it—and their insincerity roils me to no end. That said, I also don't enjoy it when a karaoke bar turns into a recital hall, one where aspiring singers try to quiet down the room so that we can stand in awe of their powers. The best karaoke nights occur when a group of random people put aside their lack of singing talent, revel in their weird musical pursuits, and perform a live-action mixtape. Imagine Sly Stone fronting the *Solid Gold* dancers in a Czech heavy-metal bar—but doing so with *sincerity.* That's what karaoke should be like, and to obtain that level of abandonment, you need a song that's not entirely campy, and yet not overly earnest. It's a difficult balance to strike.

I'm a bit biased toward anthemic, upbeat songs, as I do not have particularly evolved musical tastes. I listen to facile dance-pop and numbskull English metal and detest just about anything produced out of Laurel Canyon in the '70s or Omaha in the '00s. And even though I always use my year-end polls to laud bands like TV on the Radio or Ghostface Killah, my iTunes playlist reveals that I spend most of the year playing INXS or Fall Out Boy.

Nowhere do these tendencies become more evident than when I'm at karaoke. Let's take another look at one of the prime offenders on that wish list: "Illegal Alien" by Genesis. I realize that Phil Collins's career has undergone a critical appraisal over the past five years, and I'm all for it; he may have pandered like a desperate bellhop, but at least his pandering came in the form of songs like "Mama" or "Against All Odds (Take a Look at Me Now)." Yet even he would have a hard time defending "Illegal Alien," which is a borderline-minstrel show, complete with a fake Mexican accent and canned steel drums. Its racism may not have been intentional, but that doesn't make it any less shameful. There's absolutely no way for me to defend it.

And yet, when I consider "Illegal Alien" not as a piece of music to be critiqued but merely as a *karaoke* song, I can ignore the tequila references and sex-for-citizenship implications and lose myself in that indelible "it's no fun/being an illegal alien" chorus, which I would only allow myself to sing in a karaoke room. That's the place where all musical transgressions or perversions are absolved, forgiven, and danced away, as long they're relatively quick and hummable. People who go there don't want to hear contemplative dirges about mystery tramps and jugglers and all the other characters that appear in "Like a Rolling Stone." They want to hear the sort of intuitive numbers that retard all critical faculties and make you become an active part of the song.

"On Our Own," while far less offensive than "Alien," accomplishes this, despite the fact that it is one of the weakest of the five singles Brown released between 1988 and 1989 (though it's not as bad as "Roni," which always sounded like a slow-jam about noodles). It is a completely ridiculous song, and if it came on the radio, it would only take about forty seconds for the novelty to wear off. Yet, inside a karaoke room, "On Our Own" is essentially perfect: out of the way yet oddly familiar, strutting along with unabashed momentum and unchecked absurdity. It turns everyone around you into a slightly envious back-up singer, whereas Dylan's tune induces numbing familiarity. "Like a Rolling Stone" may be the greatest song of all time, but in terms of karaoke, it's at No. 1,278, stuck somewhere between "Moondance" and "Batdance." For once, a complete unknown.

The above guidelines have served me well over the past decade, during which I've had ample opportunities to put them to use. Yet they leave a very important question unanswered, one that's bothered me for years: What about "Sister Christian"?

Released by Night Ranger in 1984, "Sister Christian" violates several rules of karaoke functionality. For starters, it's hardly mysterious—the song has been a radio staple for nearly twenty-five years, gaining even more prominence after its appearance in the 1997 film *Boogie Nights.* And although it will certainly inspire a fervent reaction among those in the room—few people are hardened enough to resist the allure of yelling *mo-tor-in!*—"Sister Christian" has a prolonged piano intro and a thirty-five-second guitar solo, both of which threaten to slow down its momentum.

And yet I've performed "Sister Christian" at karaoke more than any other song. It's certainly my No. 1 karaoke track of all time, followed closely by the Phil Collins–Philip Bailey duet "Easy Lover" and R. Kelly's "I'm a Flirt." (I may hate the canonical rankings of the music magazines, but that doesn't mean I can't make my own.) Nearly every Village Karaoke session ended with a groggy, unhealthily damp cry of the "Sister Christian" chorus, and though that constant exposure would normally tarnish a song for me, I've never grown tired of singing it. But why? How does one song violate so many karaoke rules, yet still become the close-to-ideal karaoke song?

I put the question to Kelly Keagy, the Night Ranger drummer who wrote "Sister Christian" and who sings the lead vocals. Keagy has only visited a karaoke bar once, when he and his bandmates were taken for a night on the town by representatives of their Japanese record label (he doesn't remember what they sang, but he knows it wasn't "Sister Christian"). As such, he was unaware of the song's karaoke prestige, though he notes that whenever the group performs the song in Japan, the audience accompanies them on vocals. "The Japanese are really big on that," he says. "We recorded a live concert in 2006, and when you listen to the audience, they're singing every lyric, with broken English."

Keagy knows what it's like to be inhabited by "Sister Christian": When he first wrote the melody, it stuck with him for weeks, though he couldn't figure out what to do with it. "I'd be like, 'God, this thing—I can't shake it,'" he says. When he finally came up with the chorus, he kept it as minimal as possible, and he thinks the track's sing-along appeal is due to that simplicity. If true, this would greatly discredit my second rule of a good karaoke song—that it needs to be complicated in order to maintain the attention of both the singer and the audience. But perhaps "Sister Christian" is proof that those rules are anything but absolute. A decent melody trumps all, no matter how familiar it may be. Perhaps the reason "Sister Christian" is my favorite karaoke song is that it's the most *obvious* karaoke song.

I asked Kelly for advice about how to overcome my biggest "Sister Christian" hurdle—the guitar solo. Being the drummer, he's never actually had to worry about appearing lost on stage, as he can just keep playing through the song. So he didn't have an answer.

"What *do* you do?" he muses. "Maybe you could put some dialogue in there. Or a rap."

I'm certain he was kidding. But just to be safe, please don't mention this idea to anyone. Especially not Bobby Brown.

Adventures
in
Karaoke

Fugazi, "Waiting Room"
May 5, 2007
Brooklyn, New York

Despite my hatred of the baby boomers' self-mythologizing, I am sadly, ceaselessly over-nostalgic. I rhapsodize over long-gone events, people, and hang-outs, some of which seem more important to me in retrospect than they were in the first place. And I spend a sizable amount of my cultural-consumption time indulging in books or movies that I've already read or seen numerous times before. In fact, I'm starting to wonder if there's a connection between's one age and one's penchant for old crap: I'm now thirty-three, and I'd guess about 33 percent of my total cultural intake is devoted to back issues of *MAD* magazine and *Twin Peaks* marathons. At this rate, half the movies I see when I'm fifty will be viewed for purely reminiscent reasons, and when I'm ninety I'll spend most of my hours babbling about *ALF* to a space heater.

At the moment, though, most of my nostalgia-tripping is dedicated to music—specifically, the bands I liked in college and high school. And more often than not, this means listening to lots and lots of Fugazi.

For those who have never heard Fugazi's music, the only way to describe it is as "approachably confrontational." Between 1988 and 2001, the band put out seven albums of needling, experimental political-punk songs. The members were inscrutable and more than a little self-important, but they were also appealingly contradictory. For a group of well-read mopes, they never abandoned a good chorus. Fugazi is the only band that could get away with a song like "Smallpox Champion," perhaps the catchiest song ever written about the rape and plunder of Native Americans.

In my high school, the group was embraced by pothead metal freaks and straight-edge skateboarders, many of whom put Fugazi patches on their backpacks and played the group's *13 Songs* and *Repeater* albums from their cars during the 3 P.M. car show (a daily bit of middle- to upper-class pageantry in which everyone with cars sat in the parking lot, leaned out of their windows as if they were ordering fries, and smoked in slow motion). Most often, the Fugazi song they played was "Waiting Room," the band's best-loved track, with its prowling bassline and a scream-and-response chorus. When I hear it today, I still get lightheaded.

But because "Room" was never a hit in the real world, and the group members were always so dead-set against the commercialization of their music, I've never seen a Fugazi song at karaoke. Despite the recent revival of acts like Portishead, My Bloody Valentine, and Sebadoh, indie-rock of the '90s is still underrepresented in k-box songbooks. Even the Pixies can be hard to find, though the band is more popular now than it was in 1992, when it opened for U2. Why no one has tried to exploit this fact is beyond me: I can't be the only thirtysomething who's trying to reenact the past, and in ten years or so, I'm guessing there will be an entire generation's worth of *120 Minutes* fans brooding around the streets, all of them stuck in the throes of midlife crises and desiring nothing more than to get drunk and sing old Lemonheads songs. If anybody's going to profit from backwards-facing dopes such as myself, it may as well be the karaoke companies.

Anyway, on a Saturday night in the spring of 2007, I went to a birthday party in a moderately shitkicky bar in Red Hook, Brooklyn. My friends had hired a KJ named Colin Schiller, the cofounder of a Brooklyn-based collective named the Kings of Karaoke. Schiller is a twenty-nine-year-old native Long Islander who moved to Greenpoint, Brooklyn, in 2001, after working as a roadie for the hard-core band Vision of Disorder. He soon began hosting karaoke nights in Williamsburg, right around the time that Brooklyn neighborhood was being handed over to swells of young artists, musicians, and actors. Schiller's KJ shows became known for their in-the-open debauchery, and nights were often marked by sex, drugs, and even occasional bloodshed. "It was like some cracked-out, twisted, off-Broadway musical," he told me, beaming.

Looking at Schiller's songbook, I can see why it might incite such behavior. Not only was it perfectly narrowcast to accommodate the tastes of aging music nerds—'80s punk, gangsta rap, softrock—but it included at least half a dozen songs that I hadn't seen at karaoke before, including "Bikeage," an old pop-punk screed by the Descendents. It may not have been the widest selection, but it was perfectly curated. This guy was a karaoke sommelier.

I'd invited Mike to the party, and we sat in the bar's back garden, drinking beers and canvassing the song titles. I knew I would only get one chance to sing, and I was waffling between Steve Perry's "Oh Sherry" (an old standby, admittedly, but one that I still enjoyed) and the Misfits' "Where Eagles Dare" when Mike inadvertently made the decision for me.

"Ho, shit," he said, holding up the book. "Did you see what song they have?" He pointed to a listing at the bottom of the "F" section:

FUGAZI, WAITING ROOM

Of course, it wasn't a *real* Fugazi karaoke track. As I found out later, Schiller had used an audio program to remove most of the vocals. But it was still "Waiting Room"—a karaoke possibility so unfathomable that I hadn't even bothered to put it on my wish list. Now, I would not only finally be able to perform it at karaoke, I'd be able to do so in front of a dozen or so peers, some of whom had formed their own relationship with the song around the same time I had. These were mostly people I'd met in New York over the past few years, but I'm sure we all would have been friends had we gone to the same high school, and that Fugazi's *13 Songs* would have been the album we'd have lent each other during our sophomore year. "Waiting Room" could win over this crowd within three seconds.

And here was the problem: I could tell that Mike wanted to sing it.

He didn't say it outright, but I knew he was just as starved for new tracks as I was, and I also knew that Fugazi was one of the bands we had listened to while driving around central Pennsylvania. We couldn't *both* sing it—no KJ wants to play the same song twice, and besides, "Waiting Room" surely would have lost its charm the second time around. But this was Mike's find, and I couldn't just take a song from the man who'd introduced me to karaoke, and who'd helped console me in Japan. To pinch "Waiting Room" from him would be a selfish act, an affront to our long-held rules of karaoke decorum.

But I did. I cock-blocked his song.

I didn't do it outright; I employed some especially whiny passive-aggressive techniques, and he relented. But I did it nonetheless. And for a while, I felt no guilt. When my name was called and the "Waiting Room" bassline started up, it sounded just the way it had in the tenth grade, except that now I was the one singing. I leapt up in time with the bassline, and I hadn't leapt up at a karaoke song in a long time.

Mike's turn came shortly after mine. I can't remember what he sang, but I know that midway through, I began to feel like a jerk—the exact opposite of that overwhelming nostalgia-high I'd achieved just a few minutes prior. I felt ashamed of myself, as though I'd taken advantage of one of my oldest friends in order to impress people I'd only met a few years before. I was shocked by my avarice: When did I become so greedy that I'd actually take another man's karaoke song? If the real Ian MacKaye had been there, he would have shaken his head in disgust. Then he would have lectured me for not working at a vegan co-op.

I still look back fondly on that "Waiting Room" performance, but only because of the performance itself—not the situation that led up to it. To be honest, I don't think Mike cared that much, and I doubt he even remembers that it happened. But friendships are hard won, and delicately preserved, and you can't screw with them just so you can temporarily feel fifteen years younger. Some songs should always be a duet.

CHAPTER 5

The Empty Orchestra

THE LOGO FOR JANKARA, ONE OF THE LARGEST KARAOKE-ROOM CHAINS IN OSAKA, IS A GIANT BALL OF POP-CULTURE BODY PARTS: Ronald McDonald's mustard-colored gloves, Pac-Man's dewey eyes, Mickey Mouse's creepily fixed smile. You can see it hanging over the skyline when you pull into the city on the bullet train, a welcoming reminder that you're no more than twenty minutes away from the world's most extensive selection of Carpenters songs. It's been three years since Mike and I last visited Japan, and we've spent the past twenty hours or so trying to get from New York City to Osaka. At one point, we were delayed at a Tokyo baggage carousel, where a customs video repeatedly reminded us that we were not to kidnap local toucans and smuggle them out of the country. Woe to the American tourist who shows up in Japan with a top hat and a box of Froot Loops.

We're here to meet Daisuke Inoue, the sixty-seven-year-old Osakan who invented the first karaoke machine, and, as an accidental by-product, the entire worldwide karaoke phenomenon. Because only a handful of English-language articles have been written about

Inoue—including a mention in *Time Asia*'s list of "the 100 most in-fluential Asians of the 20th century"—I know little about him. In-oue may have inadvertently guided the past ten years of my life, but at this point I'm not even sure how to pronounce his name.

Fortunately, our talk with Inoue is a few days away, which gives me plenty of time to commit "DICE-kay EEN-oh-way" to memory. For now, Mike and I can focus on the second goal of our trip, which is to engage in as much Japanese karaoke as possible. Within half an hour of checking into our room, we find ourselves in the city's Shinsaibashi neighborhood, looking for a place to sing. When Mike lived here in 1998, he'd spent many nights in the Shinsaibashi Ar-cade, an outdoor shopping center that initially brings to mind a typical American mall, with gangs of teenagers loitering outside garish clothing boutiques. But wander around for a while, and you'll notice that many of the guys have painted fingernails and teased-out, Nikki Sixx–style hair—a severe glam-rock look that hasn't been popular in the United States, even ironically, for sev-eral years. And the girls insist on keeping their skirts short, de-spite the fact that it's freezing cold outside. One of the reasons Japanese culture is so intriguing (and confounding) to westerners is not that it seems so foreign, but that it seems so familiar—at least at first. The packaging registers with our sensibilities, but the actual content does not. Innocent-looking anime characters sprout sudden porno appendages; morning chat shows digress into screaming fits; and musicians that dress like goth metalheads sound like fourth-tier Orlando boy-band members. Shinsaibashi has that same bewildering familiarity. Just as I convince myself that it's another noisy mall, I'm nearly run down by a drunken bi-cyclist, and then accosted by a fuzzy store mascot.

Near one of the side streets, we see a barker holding a sign that reads "KARAOKE ROOM," with an arrow pointing us toward the nearest Jankara location. Our energy is finite, so rather than investigate all of the area's options, we dutifully obey the sign, eventually finding ourselves standing in front of that maniacal smiley-faced logo. The Jankara lobby is bright and clean, like that of a well-kept movie theater, and surprisingly quiet. Though there are hundreds of preening teenagers on the street, the k-box rooms are all but empty—just some college-aged kids and two Americans whose eyes are wet and waning from jetlag. The attendant hands us a small basket containing two microphones, and we head to our room, which consists of a TV, a few uncomfortable couches, and a private phone connected directly to the front desk. After calling in a *nomihoodai* order, we sing the following songs:

- Van Halen, "I'll Wait"
- Justice, "D.A.N.C.E."
- Guns N' Roses, "Rocket Queen"
- Junior Senior, "Take My Time"
- Aqua, "Doctor Jones"
- Boz Scaggs, "Jojo"
- Andrew W.K., "Take It Off"
- The Misfits, "Static Age"
- Judas Priest, "Wicker Man"
- Maxïmo Park, "Apply Some Pressure"
- N.W.A., "Express Yourself" (aborted after a minute)
- Cypress Hill, "How I Could Just Kill a Man"
- The Raspberries, "Let's Go All the Way"
- R. Kelly feat. T-Pain and T.I., "I'm a Flirt"
- Warrant, "32 Pennies in a Ragu Jar" (aborted immediately)
- The Clash, "White Man in Hammersmith Palais"
- The Wildhearts, "I Wanna Go Where the People Go"

- Andrew W.K., "I Get Wet"
- Cheap Trick, "The Flame"

I rarely partake in two-person karaoke sessions, as they demand not only stamina but also a thorough knowledge of your singing partner's musical likes and dislikes. But Mike and I have done so much karaoke together that we waste little time contemplating the songbook. He knows, for example, that Guns N' Roses' "Rocket Queen" is impossible to find in the United States, which is why he puts it in the song queue as quickly as possible. And I know that he always wants a drink after "Jojo," so as soon as I see Boz Scaggs's name on the screen, I call the front desk to remind them of our *nomihoodai* order.

Tonight's setlist is far more reliant on heavy metal and nonsensical dance-pop than usual, as we're trying to keep each other awake by screaming as loudly as possible. Ultimately, though, the jetlag drags us down, and it's "The Flame"—that mewing pledge of unwavering resolve—that ultimately knocks us out for the night. A few years ago, we would have kept going for another few hours, but we're hardly the spry twentysomethings who used to inhabit Village Karaoke all night long. Besides, tonight is just the opening act in a week-long karaoke recital. So Mike and I drop off our microphones at the front desk and settle the bill. Because there are so many competing k-box chains in Osaka, the city is a singer's market, and the room rates are relatively low. After an hour and a half of music and countless beers, our total comes to a mere $30.

The next morning, Mike and I are at the Osaka train station, stuck in a commuter rush, and we're looking for a tall white guy in bright red workout clothes and a backwards baseball cap. Thankfully, there's only one person in the station—and, quite possibly, the entire city—who fits this description: Robert Scott Field, a thirty-nine-year-old American expat who befriended Inoue a few years ago. Field is a former Triple-A baseball player for the California Angels, and in 1990 he was recruited overseas to play for the Nankai Hawks, a major-league Japanese team. He moved back to the United States after just one season, but in 1998 he returned to Japan, where he found that there were numerous job opportunities for tall, athletic, bilingual Americans (Field speaks fluent Japanese, a skill he learned in part by practicing at karaoke bars). During his time in Osaka, Field has held down all sorts of cross-cultural odd jobs, such as translating interviews for Tiger Woods and David Beckham, and arranging motorcycle rentals for Bon Jovi. He even landed a role in the 1991 film *Godzilla vs. King Ghidorah,* playing an evil android named M-11. When Mike and I meet him, he's dressed for his day job as a physical-fitness instructor, but he's more interested in telling us about a song he's just written, a potential jingle called "Little Asia." He takes great delight in showing off the city to a pair of traveling Americans, and not just because I'm paying him $200 to translate the interview.

Field and Inoue met in 2001, when both men were giving speeches for a group of local politicians. They struck up a conversation and became friends, and Field has agreed to escort us to Inoue's office, which is situated in an anonymous-looking building in the Osaka prefecture. Inoue greets us on the second floor, looking like an aging but still avid beatnik: His graying hair is pulled back into a tight ponytail, and his goatee and mustache are neatly trimmed. He's wearing a black blazer, and his red flannel shirt is tucked into his jeans. Most impressively, he's walking around in shiny, big-heeled black boots. He takes a seat on an office couch, clacks his formidable boots on the floor, and tells us his story.

Inoue grew up in Jutso, a small town just outside of Osaka. His parents owned a pool hall, which earned Inoue the nickname of "the billiard child," despite the fact that he never actually played the game. "I was too short," he remembers. "I couldn't see the balls." His grade-school curriculum included several music classes, but although Inoue took singing lessons, he didn't bother to learn how to write or read music. Whenever he had an assignment that required him to recite from the page, he'd simply cut class. A few years later, when he showed up for his first day of high school, Inoue watched as a brass band greeted the arriving students; impressed by their sound, he resolved to finally take up an instrument—so long as it was easy to learn. "I thought, 'I'm foolish all the time. What can I do without much effort?' And the drums chose me."

Modern jazz was taking off in Japan during the late '50s, opening up a new job market for aspiring musicians. Inoue gigged at night and slept during the day—often nodding off in class—and after graduating from school he moved to the port city of Kobe. The nightclub circuit there was highly competitive, and Inoue found that his meager drum skills were no match for the city's more experienced players. So he began a sideline business, acting as a middleman between musicians and club owners, and pulling together freelance players to form combos. Soon, he realized there was more money to be made if he stayed off stage altogether. "I taught four guys how to play drums, and within a week or two they were better than I was," he says. "Everybody said, 'You make a great [businessman], but we don't want you to ever play again.'"

On some nights, the Kobe club owners would bring in pianists instead of a full band, and the club patrons were often encouraged to take turns singing. Inoue saw how much money the musicians were making and reasoned that it would be cheaper to simply replace them with a machine. He drew up designs for a prototype, dictated the plans to an electrician, and in 1971, Inoue unveiled the Juke-8, the first karaoke machine. The Juke-8 was a technological mash-up composed of a bass-amp speaker, a vending-machine coin-slot device, and an 8-track cassette player. For a single 100-yen coin—less than one U.S. dollar—the machine provided five minutes of music, a length Inoue selected to maximize revenue: Since the average pop song was about three minutes long, users would only get halfway into their second track before hearing a buzzer, reminding them to keep paying if they wanted to keep singing.

According to Inoue, the word *karaoke* had actually been coined in the 1950s, during a strike by a group of Japanese theater musicians. The producers were forced to pipe in prerecorded music, so a cassette player was installed in the orchestra pit. As Inoue tells it, some unknown observer pointed out that the managers had hired an "empty orchestra," which led to the creation of *karaoke*— a merging of the Japanese words for "empty" (*kara*) and "orchestra" (*oke*, an abbreviated form of *okestura*).

Eleven Juke-8 machines were produced, and Inoue used connections to get them installed in and around Kobe in various "snacks," intimately sized bars where customers pay a flat rate for drinks, food, and a personable hostess. For the first five days, the machines went unused, which prompted Inoue to hire attractive young women to go to the snacks and pick out a song. Once they got through the first verse, they were to hand off the microphone to the nearest patron—presumably male, and undoubtedly drunk—and try to keep the music going all night. After the change in strategy, Inoue says, "the machines filled up in two days. One machine filled with so many coins that it struck a wire and smoke started coming out."

Inoue hands me one of the first karaoke 8-tracks, a yellow slab of plastic with a photograph of the Kobe Tower on the front. He had local musicians record the music, and each tape could hold four songs. Most of them were in the Japanese style known as *enka*—dramatic, country-style ballads, often about love. Once the songs were produced, Inoue had the lyrics typed up, laminated, and bound together as a songbook. By the mid-1970s, his Juke-8 machines were being installed in Tokyo and Osaka, which prompted Inoue to form his own company, Crescent. He made frequent trips to the country's inns and hot springs, driving around in his custom-made karaoke-equipment van, which was mounted with a large plastic gorilla, the company logo. When customers heard the canned gorilla roar, they came running out in search of new 8-tracks or replacement microphones. The company did so well that Inoue himself became a minor celebrity, and his likeness was used in the company's advertising materials. A poster from that time finds him decked out in a slim-fitting pin-striped suit, with a microphone in his hand and a bemused, almost apologetic look on his face. Underneath, the copy translates loosely as, "The President—he's really bad at singing."

Inoue believes the karaoke phenomenon could have begun anywhere—that the urge to perform transcends cultures and borders, and if he hadn't come up with the first machine, someone else would have. "It was just out of coincidence that it started in Japan," he says. "The whole world's the same. Everybody has the same dream. They all want to sing."[1]

---

1. Indeed, a few years after the creation of the Juke-8, a Filipino named Roberto del Rosario—presumably unaware of Inoue's device—introduced the Sing-Along System, a self-contained device that didn't reach the Philippines market until the mid-'70s.

But karaoke seems destined to have taken root in Japan, where its success was aided by a number of unique historical and social factors. Inoue himself came of age during the country's post–World War II industrial boom, a time that yielded great technological advances, instilling the Japanese people with a vigor for creation. "I was born in 1940," he says. "So I have a 1940s-type of brain." Though his Juke-8 was not a technically complex device, it was ingenious nonetheless. Much like the inventor of Cup Noodles—another world-conquering Japanese product from the early '70s—Inoue saw a basic human need going unfulfilled, and responded by putting together old technologies in a new way. That sort of restless creativity was a staple of postwar Japanese culture, and it continues today. Inoue's initial karaoke-machine formula (music minus words plus amplification) has been tinkered with and refined for years, and in countless formats. In a society that adores gadgetry, it's a perennial gizmo.

Karaoke also appeals to a number of Japanese social traditions and values, including the importance of hard work. In Japan, the ability to perfect a certain song is often viewed as proof of self-discipline, and many older Japanese try to memorize at least one *enka*. This is why karaoke bars are so popular among white-collar Japanese workers, or salarymen, who go not only to smoke, drink, and flirt with hostesses, but also to impress the boss with a song (or, if the boss isn't around, to blow off some steam after a long day of work). Salarymen are partly responsible for karaoke's increased visibility in the '80s, a time when Japan was in the midst of a nationwide economic boom. As the country opened itself up to greater trade, visiting businessmen from around the world were introduced to karaoke bars, which were sometimes used as informal conference rooms. Many important meetings from that time were no doubt conducted above a din of amateur Sinatras.

But Japan's embrace of karaoke might ultimately be due to the fact that the very act of singing—which is so self-involved, so audacious—is a joyful affront to the country's own traditions of modesty and conformity. And while these traditions have dissolved in recent years, they have not disappeared. This is a culture that still emphasizes discretion, which makes karaoke's success something of a paradox: It's a mainstream activity that, for some Japanese, nonetheless remains subversive—a way to be heard in a society that still places value on silence.

Inoue's business card features a full-color picture of him squatting down next to an enormous golden retriever named Dombei. His home is in fact overrun with pets, including eight dogs and two cats, but it was Dombei that saved his life.

In the late '70s and early '80s, several competitors began producing their own sing-along machines, and by 1986, Crescent's sales began to falter. Karaoke bars were shifting away from the 8-track format, and compared with the new digital equipment on the marketplace, Inoue's equipment became all but obsolete. He then decided to cease manufacturing equipment altogether and instead began distributing digital karaoke hardware and software. The tactic worked, and Crescent recovered in the late '80s and early '90s. But the company no longer consisted of Inoue and his gorilla-roaring karaoke van. It was now a corporation, one that relegated Inoue's role to that of a middleman. "I was once a hands-on person, putting things together and meeting people face to face," he says. "The new age was not something I was interested in. There was no one-on-one communication."

In 1993, Inoue suffered what the Japanese call *utsubyo,* a nervous breakdown. "I went into a hospital," he says. "I said, 'I don't want this money. I don't want this job anymore. There's nothing for me to do.'" He handed the company off to his brother-in-law, started taking medication, and bought a golden retriever puppy, the runt of the litter. "I'd take it for a walk and forget to take my medication. That actually made me better, because it eliminated the side-effects," he says. "My heart got stronger. I got rid of my mental problems." (This is all reenacted in a 2005 Japanese biopic called *Karaoke*, which I can personally attest is impossible to find in any DVD store in Tokyo or Osaka.)

After recovering from his *utsubyo*, Inoue had to go back to work. He'd made several ill-fated financial decisions in his career, beginning with the invention of the first Juke-8 machine. Though he patented the laminated lyric songbooks that came with the machine, he didn't patent the machine itself. Inoue's logic at the time was that he hadn't actually invented anything; he'd merely taken a trio of preexisting technologies, slimmed them down, and put them together. His family disagreed, pushing him to file for a patent, but Inoue says the paperwork would have cost him thousands of dollars. "I thought, 'Why do I have to pay so much money to do this? It isn't worth my time,'" he says. "Now, in hindsight, I think it would be worth my time."

To make matters worse, he'd made some disastrous investments during the economic boom, and when the market crashed in the '90s, his portfolio was worthless. A few months before he and his wife were about to run out of rent money, he came up with another invention, one that he's eager to show off. Inoue goes to his desk and pulls out a magazine ad depicting a shiny silver box standing on two legs, like an obedient robot. Aside from a digital readout in the center, the device is completely nondescript, and the background photo depicts an empty field of grass. My guess is that it's a white-noise machine, or maybe an especially bossy alarm clock.

"This is to kill cockroaches," Inoue explains.

Apparently, cockroaches wreak havoc on karaoke machines, burrowing inside and eating away at the wiring. After seeing so many of his devices ravaged by the pests, Inoue came up with this device, which uses a timer to emit a smokeless, roach-destroying gas. And, as an added benefit, the machine scares the hell out of rats. "It doesn't kill them," Inoue says. "But it has an odor that will make them not want to be around." There are about 10,000 units in existence, and they've been Inoue's primary source of income for the past decade. Mike asks, only half-jokingly, if Inoue might want a U.S. distributor.

Inoue now spends much of his time working with a team of rescue dogs he organized after the 1995 Osaka earthquake. "The first dog saved me," he says. "I always felt the responsibility to repay the favor." He gets up to find more pictures of Dombei, and as he digs through his desk, he asks whether we'd be interested in going to his other office, where he keeps the last remaining Juke-8 machine.

We get into Inoue's white van, where I compete for seat space with a large poodle-decorated throw pillow, and drive to an office with low ceilings and puffy guest slippers in the doorway. From a closet in the back, Inoue pulls out a red box the size of a milk crate. It's painted in a dark-red hue and includes a panel of switches, a 100-yen coin slot, and a space carved out to store 8-track cartridges. The name JUKE-8 is printed at the top.

Inoue always held on to this model, refusing to let it circulate in the bars. The microphone jack doesn't work, which is disappointing until I realize that I don't know a lick of *enka*, and that Inoue doesn't enjoy performing. Earlier, he'd told me that people needed to bring him three things in order to get him to sing: money, flowers, and a cardboard memento called a *shikisi*. I have none of those things, so Mike and I just take a few photos. I wish I could say that

I felt some sort of metaphysical connection in that office, as though there was a merger between my present and this machine's past, and that I'd been nudged here by unseen forces who love tidy storylines. But that would be stretching it a bit. In the end, I was just staring at a box. A historically important box, but a box nonetheless.

Our time is up, and Inoue volunteers to drop us off at a local train station. He sends us off in the same manner with which he greeted us: quiet, polite, wholly unassuming. He must think about how much money he lost by not patenting that first machine, but if there's bitterness there, I can't find it. "His greatest joy in life," Field tells us on the way back, "is giving his grandkids a bath at night before they go to bed, and all of them singing karaoke together."

☞

Here are a few things to do on your first trip to Japan: take a train to Nara Park, where you can feed the superbly chilled-out deer; climb a mountain in Kyoto, stopping on the way down for noodles; get your picture taken next to a statue of a *tanuki*, a mythical raccoon-like creature with a beaming grin and grossly overswollen testicles.

And here's what you should do on your second trip to Japan: Ignore all the stuff you did the first time, and instead sing a *shitlodo* (or "very large amount") of karaoke.

Mike and I no longer sing as often as we used to back in New York City. The rooms there have become overpriced and crowded, and I don't have the energy to perform Joe Jackson's "Steppin' Out" on a biweekly basis. One of the appeals of this trip was that we'd be in the one place in the world where we really had no choice *but* to do karaoke. Here in Japan, there were few work-related distractions, the rooms were plentiful and cheap, and we didn't really know anybody else to hang out with. And since I hadn't been able to fully appreciate my last trip here, thanks to my bleak, post-breakup mindset, I needed to make every drunken *nomihoodai* count. I wanted Osaka in 2007 to feel like Manhattan in 1999.

So during the day, we see as much of the country as possible, making a trip to the Hiroshima Peace Memorial and shopping at several skinny-jeans stores, both of which are humbling experiences. But at night, we sing for hours on end, ordering Suntory whiskeys and beers and selecting songs from those extensive, il-logical Japanese songbooks. We go from one bar to the next, looking for tracks we'd never find back home, like these:

- **"Bee Gees Medley"**—One of the many pleasures of the standard Japanese songbook is the availability of medley tracks, which take five or six well-known songs (plus one absolutely confounding obscurity) and combine them without regard for pace or logic. They remind me of those unfortunate Best Song montages at the Academy Awards, in which all of the nominees are crammed together and accompanied by the cast of *Stomp*. Medleys are an espe-cially effective way to appreciate the Bee Gees, as many of the group's songs can be hard to take after a minute or so, especially if you have a weak falsetto. This particular med-ley includes "Massachusetts," which I have performed in at least two countries, but never in Massachusetts.

- **MC Miker G and DJ Sven, "Holiday Rap"**—Mike often described this song to me when he lived in Vienna, and I always assumed he was making it up, or trying to will it into existence. But as it turns out, there really *was* a mid-'80s disco song in which two Dutch guys sampled

Madonna's "Holiday" and rapped about going on a summer vacation. You just have to go to an Osaka karaoke bar to find it.

• **Public Enemy, "Black Steel in the Hour of Chaos"**— There is a long-running Hip-Hop Karaoke event in New York City, one that I've always avoided, because (1) I have no inherent rhythm or flow; (2) I never know what to do when "nigga" comes on the screen. Do I sing it the way it's usually written, as "n—a"? Or do I just skip it altogether, knowing that somebody in the room is going to shout it out, and then they'll be the ones stuck explaining why they're yelling "nigga" when everybody else had the good sense to shut up? As with other race-related dilemmas, I invariably end up waffling. In this case, that means making a fake record-scratch noise and a hapless look.

• **Daft Punk, "One More Time"**—We actually didn't need to come all the way to Japan just to sing "One More Time," as it's available at karaoke bars throughout America. But much like "Sister Christian," it flaunts many of those karaoke-song rules I laid out earlier: Though the track is basically one single chorus—and despite the fact that anyone living in New York City in the early 2000s has heard that chorus hundreds of times by now—"One More Time" somehow retains a sense of mystery. I will never grow tired of hearing it, and if there's a heaven, "One More Time" is always playing in the food court.

On our last night in Osaka, we set out looking for a "snack," one of those tiny bars where Inoue first introduced his karaoke machines more than thirty-five years ago. We finally locate one on a side street near a train station, tucked so far away that I doubt I'd ever be able to find it again. The bar consists of a small, windowless room, and it's covered with framed pictures and posters featuring Yujiro Ishihara, a Japanese film star. The bartender is a red-haired Japanese woman who looks to be in her late forties. She pours me a whiskey that's nearly 100 percent water and places a small basket of cookies and crackers on the bar. The only other patrons are two salarymen, who are chain-smoking and doing their best to pretend we're not here. Neither of them seems at all pleased by the presence of two young westerners, so we try to win them over by loading the bar's karaoke machine with Carpenters songs. These don't work, nor do "Sloop John B" or "Against All Odds," even when the hostess starts playing the maracas. I have all but given up on this attempt at international kinship when Mike puts on "Linda Linda," and the two men look up from their drinks.

"Linda Linda" is a twenty-year-old song by a pop-punk group called the Blue Hearts, one of the most revered bands in Japanese pop-punk band history. The song was a giant hit and inspired a 2005 Japanese film, *Linda Linda Linda,* about a group of high-school girls who start a band just so they can play "Linda Linda" in front of their classmates. I first learned the song years ago at Village Karaoke, where I would fake my way through the Japanese-language verses just to get to the main chorus:

Leen-da Leen-da
Leen-da Leen-da Leen-daaaaa

The melody is so indelible that anyone who hears it has no choice but to repeat "Leen-da Leen-da" over and over again for days on end, and I imagine the late '80s were an annoying time to be a Japanese woman named Linda. As Mike begins to sing, one of the salarymen nods approvingly, so Mike takes the hint and hands him a microphone. His voice is faint, and he occasionally pulls away to laugh, but for a brief moment, we're all yelling the same name.

When the song is over, the salarymen return to their huddle, and Mike and I spend the rest of the evening queuing up songs until there are no customers left and the hostess has to close down. One of my favorite pictures from that night is of the hostess standing behind the bar, singing the Carpenters "Yesterday Once More" with Mike. She has a rapturous look on her face, as though she's never done this before, even though she no doubt has been singing with her customers for years. On the monitor, there's generic stock footage of a London bus, along with a few lines of lyrics, which are written in both Japanese and English. Mike and the hostess aren't looking at the TV, though, because they already know the words:

> *Every shing-a-ling-a-ling*
> *That they're startin' to sing*
> *So fine*

CHAPTER 6

A Brief and Painless History of the American Karaoke Bar, Featuring Rob Lowe, Mr. Belding, and a Hint of Scandal

Los Angeles, California

In the best episodes of *The Rockford Files*, there's always a lair, some out-of-the-way hideout that's dark even in the middle of the day and populated by informants, ex-cons, and old war buddies. As a child, this is how I imagined L.A.: a city of interlocking boxing rings and nightclubs, where everyone wore brown. So when I first walk into Dimples, a Burbank karaoke bar with burnt-red carpeting and dark wood décor, I almost expect to see Jim Garner sitting in the corner, smart-talking a goon.

In his place, I find Sal Ferraro—hair combed back, gold chain around his neck—talking on the phone behind the bar. It's almost noon on a Saturday, and though the California sun wouldn't dare sneak past Dimples' stained-glass front windows, Ferraro's wearing his aviator shades indoors, making him the toughest-looking seventy-seven-year-old I've ever met. *If it came down to it,* I think as I approach the bar, *this guy could take me.* Instead, he spritzes me a soda and hands me an old promotional calendar.

Ferraro opened Dimples in 1982, and appears to have undertaken few renovations since. The club's dining booths look as though they haven't been refurbished in years, and the rug could use a good cleaning, though it probably wouldn't help much. "I purposely keep it this way, to give it that old feeling," Ferraro says. "You don't worry about somebody spilling a drink." Because Burbank is home to numerous movie backlots and television studios, Dimples is filled with showbiz junk and totems: There's a giant King Tut in the corner, some vintage headshots on the ceiling, and a collection of outdated movie projectors in a display case. And those stained-glass windows depict not religious imagery, but the logos for Walt Disney and NBC, both local deities in their own right.

Ferraro gives me a tour of the bar, stopping first at a giant fliprack full of candid celebrity photos. Over the past few years, Dimples has become a sort of rest-stop for actors and musicians, many of whom come here to decompress after work, only to wind up performing on the brightly lit, low-elevation stage in the center of the bar. Ferraro points out shots of Kiefer Sutherland, Anthony Kiedis, Britney Spears, Charlize Theron, and an unfortunately attired Lou Diamond Phillips, who was somehow convinced to wear a giant leprechaun hat and a Hawaiian-print shirt. But the most frequently documented guest is Dennis Haskins, a.k.a. Mr. Belding from *Saved by the Bell.* Haskins is known for performing Ray Charles and Billy Joel songs, and many of his performances are archived on YouTube: If you happened to grow up watching late-'80s Saturday-morning television, you will be irreversibly jarred by his performance of Clarence Carter's "Strokin.'"

In the middle of the bar, Ferraro pulls down an overhead compartment, revealing several rows of 8-track karaoke cartridges. In the early '80s, this was the only sing-along technology available, and hundreds of tapes line the sound-booth walls. He's since updated his equipment, of course—when Kiefer wants to sing "These Boots Are Made for Walkin'," it's probably unwise to keep him waiting. But Ferraro still holds onto the tapes, and he even has the bar's original karaoke machine stored somewhere upstairs. "We keep those around," he says. "For nostalgia."

When Ferraro opened Dimples, there was no precedent for a karaoke bar in America. Nor was there really any demand for one, as karaoke was still mostly relegated to Japan, where singers confined themselves to those intimately sized "snack" bars, a reflection of culture-wide modesty. That approach wouldn't work in Los Angeles, where modesty is an import. So Ferraro merged Japanese technology with American showmanship, creating the template for a new form of nightlife, one that other karaoke bars would emulate for years to come. It was an unlikely alliance of East and West—and, like so many unlikely alliances, it began with a game of cards.

␥

One night in 1980, a Japanese businessman named Kay Takagi visited a blackjack table on the *Queen Elizabeth II*, watching as an American player named Earl Glick suffered a brutal losing streak. As Takagi remembers it, Glick was about to pull out of the game when he finally received a good hand—one he was sure he could win, if only he had enough money to double down. But Glick's remaining cash was back in his luxury suite, and retrieving the funds meant facing the wrath of his wife, who'd surely be displeased with her husband's continued gambling. Takagi, sympathizing with the man's plight, threw $3,000 on the table as an impromptu loan. Fortunately for both men, Glick won.

The next day, Glick and Takagi met up to settle the debt. As the two men made small talk, they realized they both worked in the entertainment industry: Glick was the chairman of Hal Roach Studios, the Hollywood company whose namesake founder had produced shorts featuring Laurel and Hardy and the *Our Gang* kids, while Takagi manufactured and sold 8-track karaoke machines in Japan. Glick had never heard of karaoke, and since the *QE2* was scheduled to dock in Tokyo, Takagi invited him to visit his office in the neighboring city of Yokohama.

Takagi had been inspired to enter the music business in the '60s, after seeing a concert by the Ventures, an American surf-rock band that was touring Japan. He started out as a retailer of musical instruments and records, and when the first karaoke machines began appearing in the early '70s, he began selling sing-along machines. He later developed his own hardware and software. "I knew some big force would come and move the industry like never before, and knew that it would have to do with people singing," Takagi says now. "I figured karaoke was the future."

When Glick saw those early machines, he didn't quite share Takagi's optimism. The American acknowledged that karaoke might have commercial potential in his home country, but he left Yokohama without making a deal. A year later, Takagi sent him some new cassettes, along with a few recent karaoke-machine sales figures from Japan. Glick soon changed his mind, negotiating for Takagi to bring his machines to America so that Hal Roach Studios could distribute them. The American name would be "the Singing Machine," and Takagi agreed to relocate to America to help boost sales. Often, this involved standing outside of restaurants and next to hot-dog stands to put on Singing Machine demonstrations. "Most Americans seemed to get upset when listening to someone that wasn't professional," he remembers. "There was a lot of booing." Glick, meanwhile, focused on promoting karaoke around Hollywood, where he used his studio connections to give away free machines to entertainers (he claims to have personally handed one of the earliest imports to Frank Sinatra). He also lent Singing Machines to parties, where demonstrations were put on for guests. It was at such a gathering in 1982 that the company landed one of its very first clients: Sal Ferraro.

Originally from Utica, New York, Ferraro moved to Burbank as a kid, and worked in the car business before opening a sports bar in 1964. Years later, he learned that one of the bar's neighbors was going bankrupt, so he bought the property and renamed it Dimples, after an old Shirley Temple movie. Ferraro initially used the bar's modest dance floor to host swing lessons, only to discover they drew an undesirable clientele. "Too old," Ferraro says. "They didn't drink. So I forgot about that." He considered hiring celebrity look-alikes, and while scouting for talent at a party in Hollywood, he met a Kenny Rogers impersonator who was showing off one of Glick's early 8-track karaoke machines.

Ferraro wasn't a singer—"When I was a kid, we used to get beat up if we sang," he says—but he'd played saxophone when he was younger, and practiced using a do-it-yourself record series called Music Minus One, which dropped out the sax parts and allowed him to play along at home. Reasoning that karaoke might have the same appeal for attention-needy performers living and working in L.A., Ferraro bought one of the machines, along with a collection of 8-track cassettes, eventually accumulating nearly 800 cartridges.

Since there was no video component, the lyrics were printed out in books, which posed a problem for patrons, many of whom couldn't read and sing at the same time. "They got screwed up with the music and the words," Ferraro says. "It could be quite a hassle. Some people did it, but not too well." Despite this drawback, he proceeded to flog karaoke to the public, developing a number of promotional gimmicks. One innovation was to give new patrons a complimentary audio-cassette of their performance (he now gives away DVDs instead, but for years, a sign on the top of the bar promised "FREE TAPE FOR VIRGINS"). He also took advantage of Dimples' proximity to the media industry, plugging the bar on local newsmagazine shows, and even launched his own weekly public-access program, *Showcase to Stardom*.[1]

And Ferraro made sure to fill out his waitstaff with attractive young actresses and singers from around the city who could double as entertainment on slower nights, taking turns on the karaoke machine. "Or we'd take a half-hour break and do disco or something," he says. "Just to kill the time."

Even with all of Ferraro's promotional efforts, the nightclub's biggest breakthrough didn't come until around 1987, when he finally overhauled the increasingly archaic technology that he had been using at Dimples. The original Singing Machine had been simply constructed, made up of little more than an 8-track player, a few microphone jacks, and an echo effect. But the 8-track format had been in decline since the early '80s, and there were few com-

---

1. *Showcase to Stardom* is not to be confused with *Stairway to Stardom*, an amateur-performer Manhattan public-access show that aired in the '80s. Nor is it to be confused with Chicago's *Star Performer Showcase*—nor, for that matter, with an early-'90s Orlando stage competition called Karaoke Showcase, which was hosted by Bowser from Sha Na Na.

panies producing new songs. When Dimples switched over to the compact disc and graphics format (CD+G), Ferraro was able to increase his song selection and get rid of those maddening lyrics books. Monitors were installed around the bar, freeing guests to move about on stage without having to carry around loose sheets of paper. "That's what made us really viable," Ferraro says of the changeover. "You never got lost while you were singing. I started getting the younger crowd—people who would come every night, not just once a week."

Ferraro wasn't the only one abandoning the Singing Machine. In 1987, Earl Glick and Hal Roach Studios sold the company altogether, collecting a reported $1.75 million. The company had failed in its efforts to sell the public on 8-track karaoke, and Takagi had long since moved back to Japan to run his own company. But Glick kept working in Hollywood, and throughout the '80s he could be found espousing the virtues of yet another new cultural fad, one that was just as confounding as karaoke, yet ultimately nowhere near as durable: movie colorization.

Dimples bills itself as "The First Karaoke Bar in the Western Hemisphere," a claim that's impossible to either verify or refute, for there's little documentation of the early-'80s karaoke scene in, say, Uruguay. Certainly, its quarter-century run qualifies it as the most enduring U.S. bar of its kind, a sort of sing-along CBGB; the only other venue that comes close to approaching that longevity is the Mint Lounge, a famed San Francisco nightclub that introduced karaoke in 1991. But the history of karaoke is rife with parallel discoveries, as its earliest innovators were often spread out across the world, unaware of each other's existence. And for a few years in the late '80s and early '90s, Dimples had an East Coast counterpart, a raucous Manhattan club called Singalong.

Like Dimples, Singalong's backstory involves a bit of globetripping serendipity. In 1982, a lawyer and nightlife impresario named Donald Zuckerman was working as the manager for Scandal, the '80s rock band fronted by Patty Smyth. Scandal's "Goodbye to You" was a worldwide hit that year, and during a tour of Japan, Zuckerman visited a karaoke bar with Zack Smith, the band's guitarist and songwriter. Upon returning to the United States, Zuckerman continued with his day job as the comanager of a legendary Manhattan nightclub called the Ritz. But by 1987, he'd left the club, and a restaurant he was helping put together had just gone bankrupt. "I was trying to decide what I was going to do next," says Zuckerman, "and Zack said to me, 'Why don't you open a karaoke place?'"

Zuckerman found a recently shuttered, 160-capacity Italian restaurant on 19th Street between 5th and 6th avenues, an area surrounded by nightclubs. Smith, who'd been hired to strategize, came up with the idea of hiring someone who would do more than just spin karaoke tracks—a performer who could start out the evening by playing the piano or singing, and then try to coax audience members to come on stage. "Basically, to be the cheerleader," Zuckerman says. This means that the very concept of KJing was developed in part by the guy who played guitar on Scandal's "The Warrior"—a song that, to this very day, remains a staple of KJ setlists around the world.

Singalong opened in December 1987 with a heavily promoted, deceptively well-attended launch party. "The very first night, a million people came," Zuckerman says. "Then it was very slow." Zuckerman responded by throwing lots of "free" birthday parties, in which he'd waive the cover charge for large groups, knowing they'd inevitably spend their money at the bar. This enticed young female customers, who in turn enticed young male customers, and within a few months, Singalong was pulling in nearly 2,000 people on a weekend night. "We'd play the *Brady Bunch* theme, and the whole room would sing," Zuckerman says. "It was so much fun. Totally goony. It wasn't a hip crowd, ever. . . . I never tried to be exclusive. I never had somebody at the velvet rope saying, 'You're a schmuck.' Because the hip crowd will jilt you in a split second when the next place opens. And then everybody you insulted will never come there again."

Zuckerman had media connections from his time at the Ritz, and he used them to plug Singalong on radio and in magazines— a gambit that helped draw celebrities, including many of the Brat Packers who were then terrorizing Manhattan. Robert Downey Jr. and Chad Lowe made appearances, and *People* magazine spotted Rob Lowe there twice in one week in 1988: first on a date with Fawn Hall, and then on stage, singing "I Saw Her Standing There." In fact, when Zuckerman was starting a Singalong spin-off in Atlanta, the better-known Lowe brother was going to be his business partner. "Rob had a piece of it, for promotion," Zuckerman says. "He had a band, and they were going to be our opening-night band. We had a deal with the No. 1 radio station in Atlanta to do a free live show." Two weeks before the Atlanta club was set to open, Lowe called Zuckerman from Singalong in Manhattan. "He's a little bit buzzed," Zuckerman remembers. "And he says, 'Uh, I got a problem, and I can't come to Atlanta. I got in this thing with these two girls. It's cool, but my lawyer tells me I can't go.'" The next day, Zuckerman watched news reports about the sex tape Lowe had made with an underage girl, which had been filmed during the 1988 Democratic National Convention in Atlanta. "So he bailed," Zuckerman says. "I managed to do something with the radio station, but it wasn't the same."

The Singalong in Atlanta closed after six months—Zuckerman says the mostly Baptist crowd liked to sing, but didn't want to drink—and a proposed Los Angeles franchise was nixed due to stringent liquor-licensing regulations. But the original Singalong remained open for five years, becoming so popular that Pioneer Electronics supplied Zuckerman with nearly $30,000 worth of free equipment. This was a huge improvement over the club's initial set-up, which featured homemade karaoke backing tracks: Vocals were erased using audio trickery, while lyrics were transcribed and placed on a teleprompter. But according to Zuckerman, Pioneer used Singalong as a showroom for other karaoke entrepreneurs. "They marched lots of potential club owners from all over the world through my place," he says. "And within two to three years, there were [multiple] places doing karaoke in New York."

Though Singalong and Dimples were situated on opposing coasts, they both attracted a similar breed of clientele: young, on-the-prowl urbanites who wanted to drink and gawk. But their individual fates were ultimately determined by geography. For years, Ferraro had the Los Angeles karaoke market pretty much all to himself; by the time other L.A. bars began adding karaoke, Ferraro had already spent years cultivating a loyal following, and some of those people weren't going to make the commute between Santa Monica and Hollywood. But in New York City, a bar's closest competitors may be just a few blocks away, and as more Manhattan venues started bringing in karaoke equipment, Zuckerman's profits dwindled, prompting Singalong to close down in 1992. On the club's closing night, one of the employees came out to lead the crowd in a last big sing-along number: Dionne Warwick's "That's What Friends Are For."

A few hours after first meeting Sal Ferraro, I return to Dimples and find he's taken his vintage-L.A. aesthetic one step further, dressed in a jacket that bears the logo of Mark Goodson Productions, the company responsible for *Family Feud* and *Card Sharks.* He's walking around the floor with a handheld video camera, filming the members of a visibly tipsy bachelorette party as they perform Madonna's "Like a Virgin." This is a recurring gag at Dimples: get the future bride on the stage, then surprise her with this song instead of her original choice. According to Ferraro, "Virgin" is the most-played track in the bar's history, followed by Divinyls' "I Touch Myself" and Fergie's relatively recent "My Humps." If you're a musician who's interested in making a lot of money from karaoke royalties, just write a song called "Who-Who's in My Hoo-Hoo," and let America's drunkest bridesmaids do the rest.

As "Virgin" plays in the background, I'm sitting at the bar, talking to a Teamster named Royale Edward, who has a soul patch and blond hair and is dressed in jeans and a Led Zeppelin T-shirt. Edward works as a driver on movie sets, but he's also an actor and is currently starring in a Chick-fil-A advertisement. "Obviously, I'm not fucking famous," he tells me, "or I wouldn't be driving."

Edward grew up in Seattle, where he says he once played in a band with a member of Pearl Jam, and he attended school with members of Alice in Chains. When he came to L.A. in 1987, he joined a metal band and hung out on the Sunset Strip with the likes of Guns N' Roses and Faster Pussycat. "I don't want to play in bands anymore, but I want to sing," he says. "Every day you're above ground is a good day. Every day you're above ground and *singing* is a better day."

Because he's been coming to Dimples since 1999, Edward is enough of a regular that Ferraro occasionally gives him free drinks, and the KJ usually lets him bring his own karaoke backing tracks (tonight, Edward sings *South Park*'s "Chocolate City Balls," part of his $1,000 personal CD+G collection). There's another karaoke bar just a few blocks away, but there, Edward says, "you're just another sucker buying a drink. Here, it's like you're part of something." At Dimples, he can comfortably hang out just a few feet away from Olivia Newton-John and Kiefer Sutherland, both of whom he's spotted here (along with Mr. Belding, of course). That may be the club's ultimate appeal: It's a place where a driver can share a concert bill with one of the stars of *Xanadu*. That may not qualify Dimples as a historical landmark, but it certainly makes it a cultural one.

Earlier that afternoon, when Ferraro walked me around Dimples, he'd casually mentioned that the club was soon to be torn down, the victim of the city's multimillion-dollar expansion plan. "This is all in redevelopment," he said, gesturing in the direction of the street. "I've known it for twenty years. More high-rises." He's got a new place lined up not too far away in Toluca Lake, and he'll move Dimples there in a few years. Looking around the bar, though, I wonder if its grubby charm will survive the move. Dust doesn't always travel well.

Adventures
in
Karaoke

Foreigner, "Cold as Ice"
March 15, 2007
Chicago, Illinois

No matter what sort of shameful couplet you happened to use as your high-school yearbook quote, it can't possibly be as retroactively stupid as this:

> *I went outside*
> *I've been in too long.*

That's a lyric from "Bad Shit," a song by Porno for Pyros, the '90s alt-rock group that featured ex-members of Jane's Addiction. As a Jane's fan, I tried very hard to like Porno for Pyros, and I failed. Yet for some reason, I chose this verse as my faux-epiphanous *adieu,* even though it held no great personal significance. My guess is that I saw it then as a declaration of autonomy—the opening page in some noble journeyman's diary.

Reading it now, though, I see that it made me sound like an old person describing his day at the pool. I really should have gone with "Runaway Train."

For a long time, I never paid much attention to lyrics. Though I memorized hundreds of verses and choruses, I didn't always concern myself about what was contained within, focusing instead on a song's visceral qualities: If it was loud and simple, that was usually good enough for me. This is an embarrassing admission for someone who's spent so much time listening to music, but I often worried that if I examined a song's intent too thoroughly, I'd discover some flaw that would cause the whole thing to weaken and collapse. So for most of the '90s, I favored vague pronouns, simplified love-hate choruses, and lots of grunting. As a result, I listened to a lot of bad shit.

But when I began going to karaoke, I could no longer ignore the words; after all, they were right in front of me, lighting up in any one of three exciting colors, each line emphasized. All of a sudden, songs that I'd been listening to for years had deeper, weirder meanings. "Brandy (You're a Fine Girl)"? It may seem like tropical fun, yet it's actually about maritime workaholism. OMC's "How Bizarre"? An upbeat travelogue, for sure—but also one that finds its narrator hallucinating about monkeys.

When lyrics occupy both your ears and your eyes, their meaning becomes amplified, even if that meaning was already pretty obvious. Take Foreigner's "Cold as Ice": Anyone who's heard it knows that it's a bitter breakup song. But when you *see* that last line repeated over and over again on the monitor ("You're as cold as ice/Cold as ice, I know"), you realize just how rancorous it is. Especially when you're singing it in a karaoke bar in Chicago as a duet with your girlfriend.

I met Jenny shortly after coming back from that joyless first Japan trip in 2004; she had short hair and a red striped shirt—a look that was slightly, alluringly French. So I bought her a beer, and we talked about Jawbreaker, a '90s band that was far more quotable than Porno for Pyros. She liked a lot of the same music that I did, but she was also interested in things I knew nothing about, like the works of Evelyn Waugh and "sports." We spent much of that evening coming up with fictitious racehorse names, an activity that doubles as a surprisingly accurate compatibility test. So we began dating. But for months, I refused to go with her to karaoke.

Jenny would hear about the nights spent at Village Karaoke, yet I shrugged them off, claiming they were all in the past. In truth, I didn't want karaoke to be associated with our relationship, because I didn't want karaoke to be *ruined* by our relationship. Most of my adult life had taken place in these tiny, airless rooms, and the last time I'd brought someone in, it hadn't worked out. If I eventually lost Jenny, I figured, maybe I'd finally lose karaoke, too.

It was a selfish, stubborn mindset, but thankfully, Jenny kept insisting that we go, and eventually we went to a k-box venue in Manhattan's East Village. I watched as she sang Radiohead's "The Bends" and ABBA's "S.O.S.," noticing the care she took with each line. To Jenny, lyrics weren't just disposable ornaments, and so her interpretation of each song was always far different from my own. Somehow, I'd forgotten the reason I'd become so drawn to karaoke in the first place: its potential for reinvention.

After that night, karaoke became our semi-regular weekend ritual. We'd rent a room by ourselves or with friends, and even when we weren't in the city, we'd substitute for karaoke by loading a rental car with CDs and going for long drives, singing in the front seat. There was even a moment in an Orlando convenience-store parking lot when I sat in the car, zonked on cold medicine, while she used a poorly mustached cowboy puppet to serenade me with Blur's "Song 2." Over time, Jenny somehow became more karaoke-consumed than I was: Once, when our regular bar didn't have any rooms available, she walked into someone else's room, politely introduced herself, and sang George Michael's "Freedom '90." Then she walked out. To me, that's hot stuff.

All of which brings me back to that bar in Chicago. It was called Carol's Pub, and Thursday was its regular karaoke night. Jenny and I were there to meet some friends, and because it was just before St. Patrick's Day when we visited, there were oversized shamrocks on the wall, and the bearded lump working the door was wearing a green SECURITY hat. Carol's had cheap pitchers, a $3 veal special, and a row of unsmiling chain-smokers who appeared to be paying minimal attention to the singers. It wasn't a private room, but it was about as ideal as a public karaoke bar can get. That said, I did not try the veal.

After spending some time with the KJ's songbook, Jenny picked "Cold as Ice," which had a somewhat unfortunate significance for her: A few years before we met, while employed as a fact-checker at *Spin* magazine, she had worked on a story about Kurt Cobain's unreleased recordings. While the piece was going back and forth between editors, Jenny jokingly inserted into the article a few "Cold as Ice" lyrics, which were attributed to Cobain. She requested the lines be deleted before the issue went to press, but the changes never got made, meaning there are people out there who think that the same guy responsible for "Smells Like Teen Spirit" also wrote such lines as "You're as cold as ice/You're willing to sacrifice our love." This was a major source of humiliation for Jenny, and a few months afterward, she made fun of the incident (and herself) by singing those same words at karaoke with some other *Spin* staffers.

At Carol's, Jenny chose to sing "Cold as Ice" by herself, as it had long ago become one of her karaoke staples. But just before the song came on, she asked me to come up with her; she was accustomed to private-room karaoke, and she was a bit apprehensive about performing it in front of so many people. As we sang under the shamrocks and illuminated beer signs, I couldn't imagine what the audience must've been thinking: Here are these two people, presumably in love, choosing to serenade each other with a somewhat misogynistic 1977 revenge fantasy.

But then again, they were only paying attention to the words.

CHAPTER 7

The Song Vultures

I HAVE KARAOKE NIGHTMARES ALL THE TIME. HERE'S ONE FROM A FEW NIGHTS AGO:

I'm in a k-box room in Japan, standing next to a guy who desperately wants to sing Kim Carnes's "Bette Davis Eyes." But he repeatedly enters the wrong song information, at one point selecting a twenty-minute version of the Spice Girls' "Wannabe," one in which all of the lyrics are circa-1998 jokes about Bill Clinton and Monica Lewinsky. Frustrated, he picks up the microphone and starts berating me, yelling "BETTE DAVIS EYES? BETTE DAVIS EYES?" over and over again.

Weirdly, that wasn't the scary part.

What haunted me the next morning was the song *itself.* I can still hear that phantom "Wannabe," and it sounds dreadful, recorded with tinny-sounding instrumentals and arranged with minimal accuracy. Even the on-screen lyrics were a mess, moving so fast that I couldn't see how unfunny they really were. Some people have karaoke nightmares involving stage fright or public rejection; mine are focused on shoddy quality control.

Yet these visions are grounded in an unfortunate reality, for many karaoke bars rely on impossibly mediocre backing tracks, and they can undermine one of the great appeals of karaoke: that the singer can temporarily become someone else, whether it's a specific performer or an exaggerated version of themselves. Such transformations require a certain amount of verisimilitude, which is why the accompanying music must sound as close to the real thing as possible. I've had a few karaoke performances botched by crummy-sounding backing tracks, and if I had to pick the two things in the world that scare me the most, they'd be: (2) flying sharks, and (1) the prospect of singing over Chaka Kahn's "Feel for You" with a canned-harmonica line that sounds like a wheezing lovelorn fart.

For all sorts of legal, technical, and financial reasons, the songs you hear playing at a karaoke bar were almost never created by the original performers. Accompaniment tracks must be made by outside parties, and if the songs are produced with care—if every snare hit and rhythm-guitar chug sounds just like they did it in the real version—no one should even notice that it's a copy. Cultural replication is a rare craft, but a valuable one: *Guitar Hero* wouldn't be the same if it was scored using 8-bit technology, and the *Grand Theft Auto* series wouldn't be so lucrative if its creators hadn't so lovingly approximated the sensation of running over a pimp with a street sweeper. We want our fakes to be as real as possible, which is why I love Sound Choice.

Founded in 1985, Sound Choice is one of the largest karaoke-track providers in the world, with a catalog of about 17,500 songs. Its company logo—a red cursive script that rests on a blank musical staff—has been committed to one of the dorkier regions of my temporal lobe, and if you've ever been to a decent karaoke bar, you'd probably recognize it, too. This is because whatever song that followed inevitably sounded *exactly* like the original. Rather than simply programming a few keyboards, Sound Choice has an actual house band, one that I've heard countless times but know nothing about, as it has always kept a low profile. All I knew was that the company's base of operations is in North Carolina, far away from the mainstream music industry. So I went down to Sound Choice and stole a few trade secrets.

How to Make the Perfect Knock-Off

Step 1: Go to Charlotte, North Carolina

For this is where you will find the Sound Choice headquarters, which sits in a massive industrial park. The building itself is so unexceptional that if it wasn't for the company logo out front, you might drive by and guess it was a shoe-tree distributor. Or maybe a company that makes other, larger industrial parks. More likely than not, however, you'd just drive by.

In the building's corner office I meet Derek Slep, Sound Choice's forty-five-year-old founder. Slep has gleaming eyes, a reflexive smile, and his own reserved parking spot out in the small employee lot. He started Sound Choice in 1985, and on his desk, right next to a framed motivational sign that endorses "INNOVATION," there's a computer with a ready-to-go PowerPoint presentation detailing both the company's history and Slep's own personal philosophy. He speaks of his job with plenty of true-believer fanaticism, and I get the sense he's spent a great deal of his life explaining (or even defending) karaoke to others.

Slep grew up in Sarasota, Florida, in a family of self-starters: His mother, a Chinese immigrant, ran an import business with his father, a former Korean spy. Step began playing guitar when he was twelve, and often took apart his equipment to see how it worked. What started as a childhood hobby eventually led him to enroll in a studio-recording program at Middle Tennessee State University. The summer after his freshman year, he found a job working at a do-it-yourself recording booth, where customers would pay to sing along with a backing track, then receive a cassette of their performance. Around that same time, Slep interned at a recording studio, creating instrumental music for local beauty-pageant contestants. "That's when the lightbulb came on," he says. "I'd record three-year-old girls, and old ladies. I realized, 'Oh, my gosh, this is a marketers' dream. Where else can you get a customer from three to ninety-three?'"

Slep dropped out of school and began applying for loans in the hopes of starting his own backing-track business. More than twenty banks turned him down, and Slep was repeatedly told that recording studios were for professionals, not amateurs. "That's like saying only beautiful people can have sex," he says. "But no, you can be fat and ugly and enjoy sex. And you can have a terrible voice and still sing." It was a revelation, and he wanted to share it with others, forcing them to reexamine how they felt about their own voices. Too often, Slep says, he saw "little kids going, 'I can't sing,' and becoming shy. So I had to *change the American psyche and culture*. And I knew it would take a generation." I should point out here that the emphasis on those words comes not from myself, but from Slep, whose ego does not seem to be in need of encouragement: He's the only person I've ever interviewed to repeatedly bring up the fact that he's a multimillionaire. And I've interviewed L. L. Cool J. *Twice.*

In 1985, Slep borrowed $10,000 from his brother Kurt, a chemical engineer who'd soon become his business partner, and they started setting up singing booths around amusement parks. Slep shows me a picture of one of the early studios, a small room with a pair of headphones on the wall, right below a Madonna poster. On the off-seasons, he worked out of a makeshift studio in his apartment, recording musicians in the bathroom to create instrumental tracks, which he advertised in the back of *Teen* and *Tiger Beat.* "It was like winning the Indianapolis 500 with Herbie the Love Bug," he says. "Because I was up against the professional recording studios. Whitney Houston's producers had a million-dollar budget, and I had to knock her off for about $700 a song."

Amazingly, Kurt Slep says he didn't even hear the word karaoke until the early '90s, when large electronics companies began marketing their equipment in the United States. "I'm thinking, 'What the heck is that?'" he says. "'Oh my God, we're going to be dead.' But they were just hardware people. And their music was awful, like a bad Holiday Inn lounge act." By that time, Sound Choice had its own studios and roster of musicians, so the company simply kept churning out tracks, which could then be repurposed and resold in whatever new formats emerged. "I am a song vulture, dude," Derek Slep says. "I fly around, wait for you to have a hit, and swoop down on it. I make no bones about what it is."

Derek Slep seems to view karaoke in the same manner in which a Philip Morris exec might view smoking—not as an occasional vice, but as a cradle-to-grave addiction. Sound Choice has machines at Kindercare, a nationwide nursery-school chain, and produces a line of discs made especially for funerals. Since some in the death business still bristle at the word "karaoke," Sound Choice calls the series *Songs of Comfort,* the first volume of which includes Mariah Carey's "Angel," John Tesh's "Mother, I Miss You," and, of course, "Wind Beneath My Wings" (in death, as in life, we will always be subjected to the tyranny of *Beaches*). "My goal when I started, of course, was to change the world," Slep says. "And to get that little kid who quit singing at seven to sing at ten, twelve, and all the way until he's ninety. Even though he sucked."

Step 2: Teach Yourself How to Identify Karaokeable Songs, and Learn to Hate Don Henley
Sound Choice's catalog includes more than 700 different compilations, with titles ranging from *Here Comes the Funk!* to *Super Country Party Songs 1.* There are spirituals, novelty songs, wedding ballads, and an entire album's worth of Anne Murray. A few randomly selected examples from its song library:

- 50 Cent, "In Da Club"
- Aretha Franklin, "Freeway of Love"
- "Danny Boy"
- Meat Loaf, "Two Out of Three Ain't Bad"
- Rick James, "Give It to Me"
- Jeannie C. Riley, "Harper Valley P.T.A."
- Billy Idol, "Dancing with Myself"
- Peaches & Herb, "Shake Your Groove Thing"
- Beastie Boys, "Brass Monkey"
- Helmet, "Unsung"
- EU, "Da' Butt"
- Led Zeppelin, "I Can't Quit You Baby"
- Bobby Darin, "If I Were a Carpenter"
- "Take Me Out to the Ballgame"
- Dr. Hook, "The Cover of the Rolling Stone"
- Rick Ross, "Hustlin'"
- Poison, "Nothin' But a Good Time"
- R. Kelly, "Down Low (Nobody Has to Know)"
- AC/DC, "Have a Drink on Me"
- Newsboys, "It Is You"

- Rage against the Machine, "Bulls on Parade"
- Celine Dion, "Where Does My Heart Beat Now"
- "Once an Austrian Went Yodeling"
- Elvis Presley, "Take My Hand, Precious Lord"
- "Getting to Know You" (from *The King and I*)
- The Drifters, "Up on the Roof"
- "Weird Al" Yankovic, "Addicted to Spuds"
- The Judds, "Mama He's Crazy"
- Patti Labelle and Michael McDonald, "On My Own"
- Bobby "Boris" Pickett & the Crypt Kickers, "Monster Mash"

Because Sound Choice has already worked its way through much of the pop and rock catalog, the company now mostly records either recent Top 40 hits or lesser-known "classic" songs—the ones you might put on an artist's greatest-hits album, but only toward the end of side two. "We feel like we're down to the C-level songs," says Bob Clifford, who manages the company's catalog. "'Yeah, it was kind of a cool song. I'd sing it once.'"

Clifford's giving me a tour of the premises, which include three recording studios and several more motivational posters (even in the bathroom, you're reminded of the value of "TEAMWORK"). He's dressed in khakis and a short-sleeved dress shirt, but his crests of thick gray hair are just long enough to hint at a slightly more defiant past. As a teenager in Madison, New Jersey, Clifford frequented New York City's Fillmore East, where he saw Led Zeppelin and Jimi Hendrix. In the '70s, he worked in recording studios in Manhattan, engineering albums for the likes of Debbie Harry and Laura Branigan, and hanging out with Meatloaf back when the singer was still known as Marvin Lee Aday.

When Clifford joined Sound Choice in 1999, the mainstream record industry was still fat and happy: Digital piracy was a far-off threat, and hit songs lingered on the radio indefinitely. Back then, it was easy to determine whether a radio song was worthy of being a Sound Choice song, as all Clifford had to do was monitor its progress on MTV and the charts. If the song looked like it had staying power, Sound Choice would record its own version.

But hit songs now come and go quickly, which is a growing problem for Sound Choice. In order for the catalog to stay healthy, it needs a regular influx of evergreen songs—those tracks that people will want to sing along with for years, if not decades. Because few radio hits reach that level of mass saturation nowadays, Clifford spends a lot of time crap-shooting, trying to guess a song's cultural life-span. "What you want to do, of course, is find songs like 'Baby Got Back,' 'Friends in Low Places,' and 'Love Shack,'" he says, ticking off examples of evergreen tracks. "Only the killer, and none of the filler."

To decide what songs should be immortalized in karaoke form, Clifford factors airplay, YouTube views, MySpace plays, video-game placements, and advertisements. In early 2007, he heard "1-2-3-4," a folk-pop song from the Canadian singer Feist. He fell for the song's nursery-rhyme-like verses, which seemed a natural fit for a karaoke song. "I was like, 'What a great piece of music. I would love to do this song,'" Clifford says. "But I didn't. I thought, 'There's no way. She's an indie artist from Canada, and if I do that song, nobody will know it.'" A few weeks later, he was at home watching a football game when he saw "1-2-3-4" in an iPod advertisement. "I saw that advertisement, and I thought, 'Okay, now I can do it.'"

Clifford lucked out with "1-2-3-4," as the song was practically inescapable for the rest of the year, meaning that people would recognize and request the song while out at karaoke. But perhaps more importantly, "1-2-3-4" is easy to sing, with a simplified vocal arrangement and a "woah-oh-oh" backing chorus. It's that accessibility—not chart success or clever ad placement—that ulti-mately determines whether a radio hit will be a karaoke hit. "Just because a song is No. 1 on the charts," Clifford says, "doesn't nec-essarily make it karaokeable."

To Clifford and his Sound Choice colleagues, a song's karaoke-ability can be determined by a number of seemingly random fac-tors. For example, any popular or even semipopular song from a female musician is potentially karaokeable, as women traditionally sing more than men at karaoke bars. And country songs also make for popular tracks, as they can be quickly memorized and usually don't require much vocal range. But what Clifford *really* pines for are duets, because a good duet will get everybody to sing and can even lure first-timers. "Duets are a premium," he says. "They're like prime real estate." Two of Sound Choice's longest-running bestsellers are "Summer Nights" and "You're the One That I Want," two duets from the *Grease* soundtrack.

Sound Choice also solicits online requests for songs, which means that on any given day, you can look at the company's web-site and see urgent demands for obscure Alan Parsons singles or music from the *Labyrinth* soundtrack. "People say to me every day—'Nobody else liked it, but it's my favorite song, and I need you to do this,'" Clifford says. "Well, why am I going to spend a couple of thousand when nobody else likes this song but you?" But if there's enough of a groundswell, the company can be swayed. A few years ago, for example, Clifford noticed an uptick in requests for Queensrÿche, the epic-metal band whose commercial peak was around 1990. He wasn't a fan, but many of his customers were, so Sound Choice now has a disc called *Queensrÿche vs. Rush* (Rush wins, with eight songs, versus Queensrÿche's seven).

After Sound Choice okays a song for rerecording, Clifford must then get the track approved by the appropriate publishers. This is the second most important part of his job, and the one he likes the least, as it requires navigating through the oft-annoying world of music-licensing. Songwriters control the rights to their songs, and some of them, like Alanis Morissette or Bruce Springsteen, refuse to grant permission to karaoke companies. Sometimes this is done for artistic reasons, but Clifford says that a lot of managers simply don't think the royalties from karaoke are worth all the bureaucratic hassle. "It's chump change relative to what artists normally get," Clifford says. "So they don't want to do it. Somebody like Paul Simon or Peter Gabriel . . . when you call their offices, they just say, 'No, we don't do that.' Click."

Of course, it's very possible that you've gone to a karaoke bar and performed a song written by Gabriel or Simon. It's also possible that these versions were completely legal, as many bars and KJs import discs from countries with lax copyright restrictions, or hold on to older discs featuring songs whose licenses have since expired. But the karaoke market is also flooded with unauthorized recordings, which is one of the reasons Clifford gets so frustrated by Don Henley.

Because Henley wrote or cowrote so many Eagles songs, he has the right to deny Sound Choice the opportunity to rerecord them. The problem is that Eagles songs are extremely popular at karaoke, and while Sound Choice doesn't offer "Hotel California," it can be easily obtained on the black market. This means that Henley has indirectly cost Sound Choice an immeasurable sum of money. "It's hard to know where his being an asshole ends, and his ego begins," Clifford says. A few years ago, Clifford curated Sound Choice release No. 2298: *Hits of the Don & Friends, Vol. 1,* a collection of all the company's tracks that Henley performed on but didn't write (including, in an unintended karaoke-history callback, a duet with Scandal's Patty Smyth). The very last track on *Friends* was Mojo Nixon's "Don Henley Must Die," and its inclusion is nothing short of a raised middle finger. "And you know what?" Clifford says. "He couldn't care less. But insiders got it."

Step 3: Get a Decent Pair of Headphones, and a Working Knowledge of Sabbath
After leaving Clifford's office, I walk toward one of the building's recording studios, and as I approach, I hear a brisk, ominous bassline:

> Dum-dadum-da-dadum-dadum-
> da-dadum-dada-da-dadum
> DRAUUMM!

Inside, Rick Blackwell, a tall black man in a polo shirt and jeans, is sitting on a stool with a bass on his lap, looking frustrated. He's just finished playing Black Sabbath's "Children of the Grave," which is essentially six minutes of endless bass-loop frustration. After listening to a few seconds of his performance, Blackwell tells the engineer to stop.

"It's my hardest song today," he says. "You gotta be aggressive with this shit, you know what I mean?"

A few feet away, behind a wall of glass, drummer Donnie Marshall gets back behind his kit, ready to start again. I watch them run through "Children of the Grave" two more times, and Blackwell halts both takes, picking up on some bum note that's completely imperceptible to me. But Sound Choice doesn't allow for improvisations or barely noticeable flubs with its tracks; the songs need to sound exactly like the studio versions. Unfortunately for Blackwell, this means he must play "Grave" *exactly* the same way Geezer Butler played it in 1971.

When Blackwell and Marshall eventually finish with "Children," they'll move on to a series of recent Ozzy Osbourne numbers, none of which I've ever heard of. A few months from now, once today's recordings are mixed and mastered—and after their lyrics have been transcribed and timed to appear on the screen—some of them will be compiled onto albums like *Headbanger's Hits— Vol. 15,* which places "Children of the Grave" right alongside Dokken's "Unchain the Night" and Kiss's "God Gave Rock 'n' Roll to You II."

Almost all of these tracks were recorded under the guidance of Wade Starnes, who at the moment is darting in and out of the recording studio, keeping tabs on some faulty sound equipment. Starnes has been Sound Choice's musical director since 1990 and plays guitar on many of the tracks; he's forty-six years old and lean, with a short-cropped haircut and a lush North Carolina drawl. He began playing in bands in his teens, then spent much of his twenties pursuing a record deal. "I really gave it a Gipper try," he says. "I think all of us here would share the same story. But I realized that if you want to own a house and be financially stable, you might want to get on a different path." During his early days at Sound Choice, he helped Slep create the beauty-pageant instrumentals, reediting Whitney Houston songs so they'd fit under the organizers' two-minute limit.

Starnes now handles the company's musical output, which means he spends a lot of his time listening to records, deconstructing songs so that he can rebuild them from scratch. Before the Sound Choice band can get to work on a new track, Starnes puts on his headphones and begins isolating each individual line of music, trying to determine its origins. "Every nuance," he says. "What kind of guitar? What pick-up selection? What kind of reverb setting?" Starnes can't always answer these questions himself, so sometimes he has to dig around. A few years ago, while trying to figure out how Keith Richards created the crackling guitar sound that opens the Rolling Stones' "Street Fighting Man," Starnes had to go back to a 1971 *Guitar Player* in which Richards revealed the exact type of guitar he played and the amp it ran through. And when Starnes wanted to capture the murky, druggy guitar sound on Hendrix's "Are You Experienced"—which Hendrix achieved by recording portions of the song backward—he listened to Hendrix's version and learned how to play the song in reverse. For Starnes, a classic-rock pupil, this is almost the perfect job, as it allows him to accrue countless bits of trivia about the making of his favorite records, and then get to watch as they're carefully reassembled in the studio. "I grew up on the Beatles and Led Zeppelin and Jimi Hendrix," he says, "and it just breaks my heart if we do a Hendrix track and it's not spot-on."

Sound Choice also records hip-hop and pop songs, and if those tracks happen to include samples, Starnes must locate and analyze each nicked note, even if it only appears for a few seconds. When the company recorded Lily Allen's ska-pop number "LDN," for example, Starnes had to find a recording of Tommy McCook's "Reggae Merengue," an obscure Jamaican track that Allen lifted for her tune. And since many modern-day rap producers rely on constantly updated computer programs, Starnes and his team keep track of new audio software. All of which means that just about any modern-day hip-hop song can be deconstructed (and completely demystified) by a bunch of studio geeks in North Carolina.

Once Starnes is finished mapping out a song, he has to find someone who can sing it. Sound Choice records both an instrumental and a fully realized version of each track, as the company might use the vocalized take for its licensing division, which provides music for films and television. (If a director wants to use

Willie Nelson's "Always on My Mind" in a movie scene and can't afford the original, Sound Choice will license its facsimile for a few thousand dollars.) But finding the right vocalist is not always easy, and there have been times when Starnes has found, say, a Sheryl Crow sound-alike at a bar, only to bring her to the studio and find that she can't handle Crow's phrasing and inflections. Or he might discover that she doesn't want anything to do with karaoke in the first place. "Some vocalists think they're too cool for it,'" Starnes says. "'Oh, that's beneath me.'"

Assembling studio players, however, isn't quite as difficult as finding vocalists, and many of the musicians at Sound Choice have been part of the company's roster for years. Marshall, the drummer on today's "Children of the Grave" session, has been playing on Sound Choice tracks since 1992. An R&B and jazz musician who once jammed with Dizzy Gillespie, Marshall wasn't even familiar with karaoke when he was asked to come in for his first track, playing the congas on the Doobie Brothers' "Think about Love." Within a few years, he was recording thirty to forty songs a week. "A lot of people go, 'I'm not going to do that shit,'" Marshall says. "But musicians have it tough these days. This is a good source of income." According to Derek Slep, Sound Choice musicians have pulled in yearly salaries of between $18,000 and $25,000, an income that's usually supplemented with such freelance gigs as touring and teaching.

After fifteen years, Marshall doesn't have an exact count of how many tracks he's recorded for Sound Choice, though it's most likely in the thousands—all of which he's listened to at home, transcribed with precision, and then promptly forgotten about. He's more interested in Stevie Wonder and Luther Vandross than nümetal, and although he might learn a few double-bass tricks from a Slipknot song, this is strictly for-hire work. "My like or dislike of these songs depends on how easy it is to write 'em out," he says. "By the time I get into my car and I'm halfway home, if you'd asked me what I played, I would have no clue."

In fact, Marshall hadn't even heard his work outside of the studio until a few years ago, when he took a vacation in Mexico with his soon-to-be wife and wandered into a karaoke bar. "I was walking down the hall and I went, 'Wait a minute, I recognize my playing,'" he says. It was a Bon Jovi song. He doesn't remember which one.

Step 4: Learn All the Words to Snow's "Informer"
There's a final step in the Sound Choice track-creation process, one that's overly technical, yet essential nonetheless. When I meet K'Nesha Maddox, thirty-one, she's wearing headphones and jabbing at her keyboard's space bar in loud, seemingly random cadences. Maddox is an encoder, which means that she transcribes the lyrics for every Sound Choice song and then syncs them to the music. As someone who barely survived a poorly aligned version of TLC's "Waterfalls," I can attest that Maddox's job is one of great importance to wobbly karaoke singers everywhere.

Since record labels and music-publishing companies don't provide Sound Choice with official song lyrics, Maddox often has to trust her ears. On the day I meet her, she's finishing up a version of "The Rodeo Song," a 1994 country track by Garry Lee and Showdown. Most country songs are straightforward enough that they can be transcribed with just a few listens, but "Rodeo Song" is sung in the manner of an especially agitated carnival barker, and thus requires a little more time. It also includes repeated instances of the word "fuckin'," and because Sound Choice's company policy is to avoid printing obscenities, Maddox has to go through and place a pound symbol over the offending words. "We pound the heavy hitters, like the s-word or the f-word," she says. "'Bitches' and 'hos' are never pounded. That's our little saying."

To encode the song, Maddox uses a software program that allows her to create accurate "sweeps"—those changes of color that indicate to the karaoke singer when he or she should move on to the next lyric. Each time the vocal line changes syllables, she taps the space bar, holding it down for an especially long note. To get an idea of how challenging this can be, cue up Snow's 1993 heavily syncopated reggae hit "Informer" (which just happens to be one of the most famously tricky encoding assignments in Sound Choice history). As you listen, try to tap the space bar on your computer at the exact moment Snow hits a new syllable. It's maddening. Your boom-boom will be licked down by the first minute.

Between transcription and encoding, Maddox estimates she hears each track at least two dozen times before it's completed. That's an ungodly level of involuntary song-consumption, and yet, somehow, Maddox does not hate karaoke. "I'm so geeked whenever I go to the karaoke places and I know these songs," she says. "My friends are like, 'How the heck do you know "Red-Neck Woman"?'"

I find this comforting, as I've always believed that anyone who profits from a lifestyle is obliged to indulge in it: Famous Amos should never have moved on to healthy muffins, and Hugh Hefner should still be impregnating women, even though he's in his early eighties. Maddox would be perfectly justified in hating karaoke, but instead, she celebrates it. Though that's a lot easier to do when you already know the words.

Step 5: Go Out on a High Note

A few years ago, Derek Slep noticed that some of his customers were buying Sound Choice tracks in bulk, shelling out hundreds of dollars for computer hard drives that came preloaded with songs. This should have been good news: In the course of twenty years, his predictions about the culture and psyche of the American people had indeed come true, and his back catalog was now more valuable than ever. The problem, though, is that Sound Choice doesn't actually make hard drives. Instead, these collections were being sold by karaoke pirates, meaning that some of Sound Choice's profits were going to some dickhead with a CD+G burner and a well-disguised eBay account.

Much like the porn business, the karaoke business operates in the shadow of its more mainstream counterpart. Slep may not be able to enjoy the same cultural status or wealth as the "legitimate" major-label moguls, but he nonetheless inherits all of their problems: When a company like Interscope can't produce hits, for example, a company like Sound Choice can't reproduce them. And by far, the most unwanted trickle-down effect from the music industry has been its inability to thwart digital piracy. After all, if fourteen-year-olds feel little guilt about illegally swapping songs by their favorite artists, why would they feel remorse about downloading some goofy karaoke song?

"We have had some economic tough times because of piracy," says Slep. He monitors auctions on eBay and Craigslist, and, like some of his major-label counterparts, he alerts the proper authorities whenever he sees illegal activity. There have even been some high-profile karaoke busts: In the summer of 2007, a Minnesota man was convicted of selling thousands of copyright-protected karaoke tracks over the Internet. When FBI agents raided his home in 2006, they seized more than 200 computers and storage devices and found large amounts of duped CDs.

But even with occasional government intervention, Sound Choice has struggled. The year 2006 was "a very financially hellish year," Slep says with a sigh. In addition to dealing with piracy, Sound Choice is also paying more money for licensing fees than it did a few years ago, thanks to changing copyright laws. Realizing that the company's future health would depend on adapting to new technologies, Slep sold the company's catalog in early 2007 to Stingray, a Montreal-based firm that specializes in digital distribution. Sound Choice's future now depends on finding new uses for its song catalog, whether it's licensing songs for movies or TV or developing projects like the Karaoke Channel, a twenty-four-hour karaoke network. "It's like selling one of your children," Slep says. "But in some sense, are you willing to sacrifice your leg to keep your body alive?"

It's a physiologically iffy metaphor, but I understand Slep's greater point: If he keeps trying to make it as a song vulture, he'll eventually starve.

A few months after my visit to Sound Choice, the company let go of nine staffers—including Clifford and Starnes—and announced plans to relocate its track-recording operations to Montreal. Sound Choice would keep producing karaoke tracks, but only about 600 or so a year—a meager output compared to the company's late-'90s heyday, during which it churned out as many as 1,400 songs a year. Shortly after the deal was made, I called Derek Slep, who told me he intended to keep the North Carolina studios open, so that they could be used by local musicians and advertisers. But there was a slight heavy-heartedness in his voice, and I couldn't help but be reminded of Daisuke Inoue, another karaoke pilgrim whose homegrown passion was eventually subjugated to corporate-world realities.

As a fan, I find all of this depressing. I worry that I someday I'll fall for a new song, only to discover it was never preserved in karaoke form by Sound Choice. I trust them, and I just can't sing with someone I don't trust. Performing with an unknown karaoke track is a risk, like playing a sold-out concert with a band you've never even met before. When the curtain rises, will it reveal a skilled four-piece band with all the right effects pedals? Or will it just be some dude with a drum machine and a kazoo?

It may seem like a trivial threat, but I worry about things like this. It's the stuff of nightmares.

CHAPTER 8

Horny Bugle Boys and Random Fly Girls: The Lost Art of the Karaoke Video

W E OPEN ON A BLACK MAN WALKING A WHITE DOG.
He exits his suburban home in the late afternoon, heading toward an anonymous-looking state park. Upon his arrival, he encounters another inter-species duo, one that consists of a *white* man walking a *black* dog. The two men don't address each other at first, and their cautious facial expressions hint at tension. But once the dogs begin playing together on the grass, their owners suddenly warm to each other, laughing and making small talk and playing with a camera that one of the men has. We close on the four of them strolling home together, into the sunset.

And this, according to a 1988 karaoke video, is what Paul McCartney and Stevie Wonder's "Ebony & Ivory" is all about: racist dog-lovers who cruise gay pick-up spots and enjoy photography. At least, I *think* that's what this clip is trying to convey. Mostly, it just makes me realize how much McCartney has come to resemble a Shar-Pei.

"Ebony" is one of the thousands of karaoke videos (or "karaokes") made in America during the mid-'80s and early '90s, a time when laser-disc and CD+G manufacturers were in need of attention-grabbing mini-movies to accompany their instrumental tracks. The clips were made without the original artists' input, and often directed by novice filmmakers who had to work with menial budgets and strict deadlines. As a result, many karaokes were nonsensical and distracting, which was exactly the point. The videos were intended as a performance-enhancement aid for nervous singers, who could take comfort in the fact that the audience was more interested in what was happening on the screen than what was happening on the stage.

Because Village Karaoke used vintage laser-discs, I've seen so many karaokes that I can often identify the song being portrayed before the lyrics sweep the bottom of the screen. A torpid businessman drunk-dialing from a bar? That would be the opening of Todd Rundgren's "Hello, It's Me." A sexy woman feeding geese? It's obviously "Summer Breeze," by Seals and Crofts. This is an area of expertise that few other people share, or strive for, as karaokes are among the most widely disregarded artistic media of the twentieth century. The format's short-lived heyday is either forgotten with ease or remembered with scorn, mostly because so many karaokes were blatantly, almost admirably inane. Anyone who went to a karaoke bar in the early '90s bore witness to numerous clips featuring either (a) stock footage of yachts; or (b) stock footage of couples taking pre- and post-boink walks on the beach. So when karaokes began to disappear around the turn of the century, nobody mourned their loss.

Except for me. I've been trying to build an archive of these videos for years now, ever since Village Karaoke closed down. This is partly due to that lame tug of nostalgia, as I wanted to re-create those early karaoke days at home. But I also wanted to preserve what I saw as a languishing art. Granted, a lot of the old karaokes are terrible and can only be appreciated from a safe, ironic distance. But there were clips that transcended the limitations of the form, and creators who re-imagined popular songs in ways I never would have conceived. Unfortunately, most of these golden-era karaokes have long gone out of circulation, replaced by cheaper CD+Gs that often consist of nothing more than a few brightly colored lines of text. There's no karaoke-industry archive to preserve them, and no VH1 Classic Karaoke channel pumping them out for new audiences to discover. For years, I had no way to see those old clips again, except to rent out a room and hope it hadn't updated its technology in ten years.

In the spring of 2007, however, I noticed an ad on Craigslist offering an entire crate's worth of out-of-print karaoke laser-discs for a mere $200. Fearing that some other Brooklyn-based karaoke-video obsessive would scoop up this mother lode, I immediately called the seller, offering to pay full price, in cash, that very same night. He was a KJ phasing laser-discs out of his act, and though I was grateful to relieve him of his archive, I couldn't quite figure out why he'd waited until now to dump such an obsolete technology. I imagine his other Craigslist sales consisted of VHS rewinders and war bonds.

Once the crate arrived, I began pulling out the discs one by one and scanning their tracklists. There were nearly fifty in all, some of them blatant duds, like the all-children's volume, or the horrifically titled *Celine II/Bryan Adams & Rod Stewart* collection. Yet there were dozens of videos that I remembered from Village Karaoke. For weeks, I watched those clips at home, where the combination of fuzzy-headed reminiscing and sparse musical arrangements had an occasionally narcotizing effect (I once fell asleep on the couch, only to be awoken by a vocal-free version of Milli Vanilli's "Blame It on the Rain"). Instead of singing along, I took notes, and after a while I began noticing themes and archetypes that were common to all of these videos, even though they'd been produced over the course of several years by a variety of companies and filmmakers. For example, most of the karaoke videos in my collection include at least *one* of the following characters:

- The Wandering Lover: By far, the most frequently recurring karaoke-video storyline revolves around two distraught ex-paramours who spend their time taking walks alone and frowning at nature. Such clips usually end with a reconciliatory hug on the boardwalk, and I'm now convinced that the people I often see staggering around Venice Beach in old sweatshirts are not actually bums, but karaoke-video actors who have been staying in character since 1989.

- The Soft-Core Swooner: The couples who aren't separated and sulkily roaming around the streets alone can be found taking horseback rides together, sitting in hot tubs, or generally just rubbing up against each other in slow motion, like on the first three minutes of every episode of *Silk Stalkings*. Though I've never seen an American karaoke video that includes nudity, a few of them do possess a certain could-be-a-butt ambiguity.

- The Random Fly Girl: Karaoke-video directors cribbed from all sorts of outside influences, from *Fame* to *West Side Story* to Janet Jackson's "Pleasure Principle" warehouse-dance. But mostly they tried to copy the hot-pink aesthetic made popular by *Club MTV* and *In Living Color*, which makes for constant interruptions by women wearing neon-colored baseball caps and doing the Hammer Dance. This style is especially conspicuous when it's paired with an old song, such as the Monkees' "Last Train to Clarksville."

- The Horny Bugle Boy: Because many of these clips were made at the tail end of the Reagan era, they reflect that period's rampant, tackily unaware consumerism. In fact, some karaokes don't include a story at all: They're just '80s-style male fantasies, set in a world where polo shirts are always tucked into khakis and blondes are always poured into Ferraris. In such clips, the guys seem to be primarily concerned about sex and status, and in real life, most of them would probably wind up as oft-wandering lovers.

- The Guy Who Picks a Random Woman Off the Street, Puts Her on the Back of His Motorcycle, and Then Takes Her to a Farm So That They Can Dance Near the Rail Yards: Is this actually a recurring female fantasy? If so, I don't quite get it. Wouldn't the ride home be awkward?

As I watched these discs, I noticed several innovative and unpredictable videos hidden among the goofier, more conventional ones. There's a trippy version of Gary Wright's "Dream Weaver," for example, in which the song is re-imagined as a sort of psychedelic *Top Gun*, complete with an upper-atmosphere fantasy sequence. And there's an oddly moving gospel clip that follows a group of slow-moving, almost spectral dancers around a misty cornfield. Granted, a lot of the videos are clunkily literal, such as the version of Garth Brooks' "Friends in Low Places" that focuses on a cowboy dwarf. But many of the clips are distinctive enough to merit repeat viewings.

More often than not, the clips I wound up watching the most all bore the same company logo: Pioneer. In the '80s and early '90s, when the company was still manufacturing laser-disc players, Pioneer hired studio musicians and commercial directors to create karaoke videos, which were placed on compilations that retailed for as much as $150 a pop. "The margins were huge," remembers Bud Barnes, a former Pioneer marketing executive. "It was the old razorblade-razor story: If you could get the hardware into the market, the software drove the profit." Pioneer gave directors budgets in the low-to-mid four-figures—a tragic figure for a *real* music video, but extremely generous for karaoke.

As I worked through my initial crate of laser discs, I became fascinated with the Pioneer oeuvre. I started buying new volumes on eBay whenever I could, to the point where I spent $40 just to locate one Bon Jovi clip. As far as I'm concerned, the Pioneer videos are underappreciated works of art, each one the product of a singular—and often absurd—vision. But whose visions were they, anyway?

In 1986, Jim Gerik was working as a music-video director in Dallas, where he filmed clips for the likes of Amy Grant and the Marshall Tucker Band. While attending a local lighting designers' convention, he met representatives from Rock Video International, a New York–based company that was demonstrating its line of karaoke videos. "To see people singing with a screen and words," Gerik says nearly twenty years later, "I thought it was strange." The clips were shot on 16mm film and exported back to Japan, and while Gerik didn't care for the work the company had done so far ("cheesy storylines," he says), he was impressed by its budgets, which Gerik estimates were about $4,200 per video. He excitedly began pitching them ideas, and a check for $15,000 arrived a short while later. "They said, 'Here's a start,'" Gerik remembers. "I had to figure out how to do it."

Because the costs of processing 16mm film threatened to eat up much of that first check, Gerik planned the shoots as thoroughly and cheaply as possible, exploiting every available resource with Roger Corman–like efficiency. He hired local models for his cast, getting them at little or no cost, since most of them were just trying to get on-camera experience. And he often improvised on the set: Once, while working on a scene that normally would have required an expensive lighting rig, he simply turned on his car's headlights.

After creating more than 100 clips for Rock Video International, Gerik was approached by Pioneer. His new client offered a higher budget (around $6,000 per clip), as well as stateside distribution, and both of these factors prompted Gerik to reevaluate his approach. American viewers had become accustomed to lavishly produced music videos, and Gerik knew that a cheaply lit karaoke clip wasn't going to impress anybody who'd seen the likes of Peter Gabriel's "Sledgehammer." So Gerik and his production company, Tocrok, began hiring directors from around the region, instructing them to use MTV for their ideas. Sometimes, this meant copying imagery from specific videos, such as when Gerik paid homage to Robert Palmer in a "Jingle Bell Rock" clip by surrounding Santa Claus with a kickline of glum, tight-haired female musicians. But usually, the directors used traditional music videos as a source of inspiration, trying to re-create their effects, their elaborate camera work, and their multicharacter narratives on a limited budget. One clip that Gerik is especially proud of is a cinematic version of Bon Jovi's "Wanted Dead or Alive," which follows a group of battling cowboys, including one whose gun magically transforms into a guitar. The video shoot included not only a fake-blood squib effect, but also a few dangerous-looking falls; amazingly, Gerik found a few aspiring stuntmen working in his office building and got them to work free of charge. The squib didn't fire exactly as he'd planned, yet the video remains a favorite of Gerik's. "I went, 'Wow, this looks cool,'" he says. "'It's just like a little movie.'"

Pioneer came to Tocrok with "batches"—random sets of songs that could include anything from country to R&B to even children's music. "We'd think, 'Jeez, what am I gonna do for *this* one?'" he says. "In your mind, you gotta get creative, or drunk, or both." At the company's early-'90s peak, Gerik was producing nearly 130 videos a year, traveling around the world to collect footage. He'd learned to pick up a camera even when he was off the clock and mine every location for possible material; once, while on a trip to Mexico for a non-karaoke client, he found enough downtime to shoot at least five different videos.

When I spoke to Gerik in the spring of 2007, it had been more than fifteen years since he had filmed his last karaoke video. The job had been lucrative, but not exactly prestigious. "The *Dallas Morning News* wanted to do an article on me, and I was like 'Hell, I don't want people to know what I'm doing!'" he says. "The concept kind of embarrassed me, to be honest. If there's a low end of the film business, that would be it. But I didn't have the perspective to see what we were doing." Today, Gerik shoots commercials and industrials, using many of the same on-the-fly methodologies he learned from working on the Pioneer gig. "I base a lot of it on the karaokes," he says.

Gerik produced or directed nearly 500 videos in the '80s and early '90s, and indeed, his credit can be found on many of the Pioneer discs. Another name that pops up frequently is Paris Barclay, a television and music-video director who won Emmys in the late '90s for his work on *NYPD Blue,* and whose credits include episodes of *Lost, The West Wing,* and *ER.* In the early '90s, Barclay ran Black & White Television, the production company responsible for such music videos as L. L. Cool J's "Mama Said Knock You Out." Pioneer approached Black & White about karaoke batches, offering around $5,000 to $6,000 per video. "It was largely to help directors without work who needed to show something," he remembers. "My company could then take the work around and demonstrate what they could do on a small budget." According to Barclay, one of the filmmakers who directed karaokes for Black & White was former *Cosby Show* star Malcolm-Jamal Warner.

Like Gerik, Barclay espoused the virtues of quick, economical shoots. Directors only had four rolls of film, and Barclay would often work at a moment's notice (he once filmed a video while vacationing in Hawaii). For Madonna's "Live to Tell," Barclay, using his brother's house as a location, created a mini-thriller in which a murderous husband is discovered by his too-curious wife; it ends with her body being buried in the backyard. "Still my favorite of all my karaokes," he says. "Live to Tell" was thematically grim, but it wasn't explicit: Pioneer had to sign off storyboards before a shoot could begin, and it forbade its directors from including graphic sex and violence, as the videos might offend its customers overseas. Otherwise, the filmmakers were usually allowed to explore whatever ideas they had, so long as those ideas didn't cost too much money or take up too much time. According to Norry Niven, another Pioneer video director, the company gave directors "quite a bit of control, unbelievably. For me, that was the big appeal—the control, and the opportunity to go out and shoot cool stuff. Certainly, we weren't doing it for the financial gain."

Because so many Pioneer videos were shot in major cities like Los Angeles, New York, and Dallas, they provided entry-level work for then-struggling performers. Barclay hired Dylan Mc-Dermott to direct a "very dramatic" version of Buffalo Springfield's "For What It's Worth"; Gerik cast future Dixie Chicks member Martie Maguire in a clip for the Doobie Brothers' "Black Water"; and Niven worked with future *Baywatch* star Brooke Burns on a shoot. I'm positive that one of the supporting actors from *The Wonder Years* appears in a video for David Bowie's "Modern Love," though I've never been able to find it again, and none of my friends believe me, no matter how much I try and convince them otherwise. That clip is the Canadian girlfriend of karaoke videos.

The karaoke directors often went on to work in commercials, television, and music videos, and Niven even directed a short film for Showtime called *Karaoke Knight,* starring Jeffrey Ross as a lonely karaoke lover. But the most intriguing post-karaoke-video career belongs to Jay Roach, the director of the films *Austin Powers* and *Meet the Parents*. His credit can be found on a 1992 clip for the Barbra Streisand–Barry Gibb duet "Woman in Love," though you'd have to read the fine print on the back of the laser disc to see his name (and you'd have to corner him at a karaoke recovery group to even ask him about it, as Roach's publicist didn't respond to requests for comment). Karaoke-video directors rarely, if ever, got to see their names on screen.

Gerik and Barclay had both exited the karaoke-video market by the early '90s, though Niven kept producing videos for Pioneer until 1996, when the company slashed production budgets (once the laser-disc market died out, Pioneer stopped making karaokes altogether). "I think they came to the realization that no one cares," says Niven. "'We'll just put the words up there, and it'll be

fine.' And sure enough, they were right." During a trip to New Or-
leans, Niven walked down Bourbon Street and saw one of his
videos playing in a bar, where the performers were all but ignoring
it. "They're up there, singing their hearts out," he says with a laugh.
"No one cared what we were doing. But we did."

To get an idea of the Pioneer filmmakers' inventiveness, imagine a
scenario in which the estate of Frank Sinatra asks you to create a
video concept for "My Way." Don't bother questioning the proba-
bility of such a scenario; just assume that Sinatra watched *Brew-
ster's Millions* before dying and then loaded his will with all sorts
of shit-crazy posthumous tasks. The video must depict your idea
of what the song *means*—that is, you must try to replicate on-
screen whatever images happen to come to mind when you hear
the song. There are a few stipulations:

1. Your video cannot borrow from or even reference
   another person's vision of the song.
2. Your video can't include copyrighted footage of Sinatra,
   or his ghost will come back and break your nose with
   a tumbler.
3. Your video has to be cheap enough that it can be filmed
   within one or two days.
4. Your video can't contain any nudity or violence. All
   thongs must be at least one inch wide.

That's an imposing list of rules, and yet some directors for several
competing companies often worked under similar restrictions.
Here's how three of them interpreted "My Way":

"My Way" Version #1

Synopsis: No actors, just a montage of white-water rapids, with the waves growing more dangerous as the lyrics become more despondent. By the end, the rivers have grown into waterfalls, which crash on the rocks and run beneath tall pedestrian bridges.

Concept: "My Way" as suicide note.

"My Way" Version #2

Synopsis: A surfer in his early twenties takes a daylight drive around a coastal city. He walks along the beach, staring at the ocean and repeatedly running his hands through his hair. After changing clothes, he walks along a different beach, and then gets back in his car and drives home.

Concept: "My Way" as excuse for navel-gazing introspection.

"My Way" Version #3

Synopsis: Sitting alone at a bar, a nattily dressed older gentleman smokes a cigar and watches a young couple dance. The clip is filmed mostly in black and white, but it's interrupted by sepia-tone footage of another couple dancing in flashback—presumably the old man and his former lover.

Concept: "My Way" as bittersweet nostalgia trip.

The first "My Way" is by far the most unsatisfying, as its outdoor scenery, while intended to be calming, is actually so repetitive that the song seems to go on forever. And there's no indication that all these rivers and waterfalls were filmed specifically for the song—it's just a collection of stock nature footage, and I'm certain it was cannibalized for later videos. At least the second clip makes an attempt to depict the song's message of isolation, even if it does so without a sense of purpose: We don't know who this guy is, or why he's always on the beach. It seems like a typical wandering-lover clip, yet we don't know why he's wandering, or if he's even in love with anybody, aside from himself.

The third clip is from Pioneer, and it was obviously created just for "My Way"—there's even a dramatic cigar-smoke exhale timed to the "I did it all" finale. Admittedly, the video's storyline is pretty slight, and it takes a sort of creepy turn toward the end, when the old man appears to be murmuring to himself. But at least this version *has* a storyline, not to mention high-grade production values, having been shot on film rather than video, and edited with enough care that the bittersweet tone remains consistent throughout. With the exception of the lyrics running in hot pink across the bottom of the screen, it doesn't really look like a karaoke, which is what makes it so effective: If the purpose of a karaoke video is to distract the audience from the singer, then a clear-cut narrative—even one that's centered around a dying old man—is going to be far more compelling than a bunch of crashing waves or some forlorn surfer.

What I like most about this clip, however, is not its utility, but its idiosyncrasy. Everyone has a different interpretation of "My Way," and the Pioneer clip takes one such vision and translates it for the screen with clarity and precision. This is what "real" music-video directors do all the time, of course, with one exception: Their version must be made with the artist's cooperation, even if it's minimal. There's nothing in the lyrics to ZZ Top's "Legs," for instance, to imply that the song is about a hallucinating shoe salesman. Yet that's implied in the official video, and even if the band members didn't come up with that idea, they at least endorsed it. "Legs" reflects their concept of what the song is *about*, and that's one of the reasons I always hated music videos: I didn't like being told that my understanding of a song was somehow incorrect.

In this way, karaoke videos are more *pure* than their MTV counterparts. There's no filtering or direction from the artist, and absolutely no insight as to what might have inspired the song. Karaoke directors were free to carry out the song's ideas in ways that the songwriters could never have guessed—or maybe even approved—and that's why I can still watch the Pioneer videos outside of the karaoke room. They illustrate that one piece of music can hold thousands of meanings, even weird ones.

In fact, I'm still looking for a copy of the oddest karaoke video of all, one that I saw many times at Village Karaoke: Pioneer's take on Elton John's "Bennie & the Jets." For years, the clip made no sense to me, as it begins with a group of preteen kids playing musical instruments on stage, and ends with them walking down a hallway toward a creepily grinning housewife who's luring them with a plate full of chocolate-chip cookies. There's no Bennie, no jets, and no electric boots and/or boobs. I always held "Bennie" up as an example of the most random karaoke video ever made, until I realized that the opening lines of the song were "Hey, kids." Using just those two words, somebody came up with that baffling storyline, one that's a bit of a stretch, but nonetheless unique. It's something no one else in the world could possibly have come up with, even if they were drunk, or creative, or both.

Adventures
in
Karaoke

Prince, "Raspberry Beret"
April 14, 2007
Brooklyn, New York

I'm standing outside of a nightclub on a Saturday night, waiting for the doors to open, when a voice behind me begins singing Seal's "Kiss from a Rose." I know it's not Seal himself, as the voice is distinctly feminine, and besides, Saturday night is when he and Heidi Klum take turns exfoliating in their grotto, which is carved from scented candles and filled with heated aloe. When I turn around, I see two men and a woman standing against the wall, harmonizing. They all appear to be about a decade younger than me, and clearly have no compunctions whatsoever about the fact that everyone in line can hear them. I keep my head forward, even when the song grows so loud and pervading that I expect it to take a physical form and tap me on the shoulder.

The club is called Studio B, and the headlining act tonight is Of Montreal, a new-wave art-rock band from Athens, Georgia. The group doesn't have a large following outside of indie-rock circles, but you may have heard its music on a recent Outback Steakhouse commercial, in which the lyrics "Let's go Outback tonight" are cooed over a supple bassline and close-ups of a Bloomin' Onion; it's certainly the most sexually suggestive restaurant-chain jingle since "There's Nothing Like the Whopper." Of Montreal is playing two sets tonight, the second of which is billed as "indie-rock karaoke," where audience members will fill in for the band's lead singer. I couldn't imagine such an ostentatious event taking place ten years ago, when alt-rock fans were by and large a group of self-righteous, miserly introverts. But Of Montreal's fanbase skews young, and many of its followers were in their late teens during the teen-pop/*Idol* era, so the concept of indie-rock karaoke probably doesn't strike them as odd.

Figuring there'd be no shortage of volunteers, I enter the club and walk straight to the sound booth, looking for somebody with a clipboard. The song selection is a mix of alt rock and classic rock, and I put my name next to Pavement's "Cut Your Hair," a '90s indie hit that I've been hoping to find for years. I'd come here tonight mostly for this one song, and though I'm relieved to claim it, I'm less enthusiastic about scratching it off my karaoke wish list in front of about 500 people. I thought I'd long ago conquered my stage fright, but as I walk around the club—which is certainly the largest place I've performed since that gay thunderdome in the Hamptons—I pine for the cowardice and solitude of my early twenties.

Toward the front of the stage, I see the trio of Seal fans and introduce myself. The female voice I'd heard earlier belongs to Monica DeTonnancourt, a nanny who lives in New Jersey, and who spends her weekends crashing on friends' couches in New York City. DeTonnancourt is wearing a blue bandana printed with skulls, a black blazer, and—in a nod to Of Montreal's love of ornate costumes—a thin, hand-drawn mustache over her lips. She's here with Jon Anzalone, a photographer wearing a headband and sunglasses; and Fred Arnold, a college student dressed in a pin-striped blazer over a shirt and tie. Anzalone and DeTonnancourt met a few years ago online, and the three of them became friends while driving from New York City to Athens in the summer of 2006 for a music festival. "We've been concert buddies ever since," DeTonnancourt says.

The three of them have very little karaoke experience, which surprises me, given their penchant for busting out adult-contemporary ballads. "I just never found the right time or the right place or the right people to come with," DeTonnancourt says. The closest she got was a few nights before the concert, when she and a friend had been sitting in a bar as a Prince song came on. "We just looked at each other, and we were like, '*Rasp-ber-ry Ber-et*,'" she chimes. "We got all the people to sing."

Tonight, she's signed up for Boston's "More Than a Feeling"—her first choice, Journey's "Don't Stop Believin'," had already been claimed. Her friends are planning a duet of the Pixies' "Here Comes Your Man." These choices all made sense a few minutes ago, but now, as the club begins to fill, I can tell they're getting nervous. So I offer a few public-karaoke guidelines: (1) Make sure your friends stand in the front, so that they'll always be in your eye line; (2) if you must flail, do so vertically, not horizontally, so that you won't backhand the keyboardist; and (3) when you inevitably forget the words, just string together some nonsense in a reasonably melodical way, like the guy from Dexy's Midnight Runners.

DeTonnancourt, however, has her own strategy, one that seems to contradict nearly forty years of karaoke tradition. "I'm not gonna drink, for fear of getting sloppy drunk," she says. "I can't disrespect Boston."

The members of the Sudden Seal Trio all seem like good eggs, and yet I can't watch Of Montreal with them. They're all in their early twenties, which means they're still young enough to camp out near the front speakers, while I prefer to spend most live shows hunched over by the exit, calculating how much set time is left before I can go home. My enthusiasm for live music has waned in the past few years, and I can't help but wonder if karaoke is to blame: After a half-hour or so of watching a band's performance, I inevitably realize that I'd be having more fun if I could just sing the song myself. So I leave the three of them and head to the bar, where I promptly ignore DeTonnancourt's advice.

Shortly after Of Montreal's official set, I'm in a waiting area by the side of the stage, finishing off yet another ennobling whiskey. I've been watching the last few songs from here, which was a mistake, as seeing the crowd from the band's perspective only brought the audience's magnitude into greater relief. The karaoke portion of the evening is hosted by Michael Showalter, a comedian who performed as part of an early-'90s comedy troupe called the State, and who starred in the film *Wet Hot American Summer.* He introduces a guy dressed as Aquaman, who performs David Bowie's "Moonage Daydream," and I begin to wonder if "Cut Your Hair" will make me look like a weenie. After all, these people have just watched an aquatic superhero do a glam-rock song, and I'll be walking on stage in a corduroy blazer and jeans, singing a tune with a chorus that consists of dainty little "oooh ooh oohs." As I contemplate whether to skip out, I see DeTonnancourt coming toward me, frowning under her fake mustache.

"Paul Rudd just stole my song," she says.

To be clear, I don't think Paul Rudd *actually* stole "More Than a Feeling" from her. My guess is that he was invited by Showalter— with whom he starred in *American Summer*—and was told to sing whatever he wanted. To this day, he probably remains unaware of the fact that he was, in effect, pooping down a well that was filled with someone else's hopes and dreams.

"What if we sang 'Raspberry Beret' together?" I ask.

The song seemed like the perfect solution to our problems: DeTonnancourt would still get a chance to sing with Of Montreal, and I'd be able to get out of the Pavement song. Plus, neither one of us would be up there by ourselves; we could just be sidekicks for each other. "Raspberry Beret" would fix *everything*. It always does.

DeTonnancourt is unsure about this decision, as she only knows the song's chorus. But all of her other choices have already been taken, so we spend the next ten minutes at the bar, practicing "Raspberry Beret." As we rehearse, Rudd handsomely walks into the club, and Monica excuses herself to trail him through the crowd. I find this a bit troubling, as I've only met this woman tonight. Is she the kind of person who would take a swing at Paul Rudd?

She places herself between Rudd and the stage and says a few words to him, though the only ones I can make out are "Good luck." When she turns around, he bends his eyebrows and makes a half-smile, a look that indicates confusion, yet does little damage to his seemingly unflappable handsomeness. Clearly, he has no idea why he was just confronted by a woman with a hand-drawn mustache.

"I said, 'Please just do Boston right,'" DeTonnancourt tells me.

We practice "Beret" one last time, and then watch as Rudd and comedian David Wain sing "More Than a Feeling." Even though it's a slightly hokey classic-rock anthem being performed by two comics—one of them so very, very handsome—the performance is unexpectedly poignant: Boston's lead singer, Brad Delp, had committed suicide only a few weeks before, and hearing two people repeatedly fail to hit his trademark upper-register notes somehow makes his death seem more affecting.[1]

---

1. A year after the Of Montreal concert, Boston hired a new lead singer, who was discovered when the band heard him performing over karaoke tracks online. That singer was not Paul Rudd.

DeTonnancourt and I are slated to go up next, and I'm hoping the crowd will be so keyed up on a mix of celebrity-vicinity delight and remember-the-dead sentimentality that we can coast on their residual goodwill.

Our names are called, and DeTonnancourt and I take to opposite ends of the stage. As Of Montreal begins playing, I give her an encouraging nod, which she mistakes for her cue, and jumps early into the first line. The band adjusts accordingly, however, and as the song proceeds, the two of us trade verses back and forth, to the point where the performance begins to feel natural—so natural, in fact, that I don't even notice that the guitarist behind me is wearing a giant pair of angel wings. By the end, DeTonnancourt and I are dancing, though how exactly you'd categorize this dance—part strut, with a hint of jig—I have no idea.

We walk down the stairs into the waiting area and share a quick congratulatory hug, after which two men approach DeTonnancourt and ask her if she'd like to sing with them. A few minutes later, she's back on stage, singing "Dancing Queen" with two complete strangers.

After DeTonnancourt and I finish, I head to the back of the club, feeling winded. I stare at Paul Rudd for a few moments—because of his handsomeness, yes, but also because he may be the only person here older than me—and then watch DeTonnancourt's two friends perform "Here Comes Your Man." It quickly becomes shambolic: A couple of women come up on stage and dance behind them, and Arnold removes his clothes until he's stripped down to a vest and pants. Just when it seems as though the performance has completely come undone, the two men halt the Pixies number and start another song, one that several people around me recognize immediately. And so begins the second version of "Kiss from a Rose" of the night, though this one is even louder, as the voices in the audience build into a serene and accidental choir.

CHAPTER 9

The Polish Guy Is Singing in the Buffet

Bangkok, an Oriental City

What does one pack for an international karaoke contest?

Khakis?

Mescaline?

Taser(s)?

It's the fall of 2007, and I'm about to fly to Bangkok for the Karaoke World Championship (KWC), a four-year-old competition that's organized by a brood of Finns and attended mostly by Asians and Europeans. I should be better prepared, as this will actually be my *second* KWC-related trip: In 2006, while on assignment for *Wired* magazine, I watched the event take place on a $200 million cruise ship that pinged between Finland and Estonia. The passengers that year may have been a bit wobbly—a condition attributable to both seasickness and the presence of an on-board liquor store—yet many of the contestants were genuinely talented, having survived a series of local, regional, and national elimination rounds to make it to the finals. (One of the Finnish singers even went on to win his country's version of *American Idol*, and later recorded a best-selling heavy-metal album.) But the 2006 competition drew nearly forty-five singers from seventeen different countries, and when that many nations get together for something as demonstrative as karaoke, certain cultural quirks tend to become more pronounced, especially in close quarters. By the time a Russian woman got on stage and sang "Feelings," all the while dressed in Barbra Streisand's *Yentl* costume, I was ready to disembark.

The Karaoke World Championship organization was formed in 2003 by Kari Hujanen, a Finnish high-school gymnastics instructor and karaoke fan. The group boasts a modestly sized staff, with many of the senior positions filled by Hujanen's own family members. The 2007 competition marked the first time the group was holding the event outside of Finland, and I had high hopes for this year's trials, not only because they would take place entirely on dry land, but also because they'd include some American contestants. Thanks to some bureaucratic mix-ups and a few alleged bungles, the U.S. team never made it to the 2006 competition, but now there were a pair of American contestants on their way to Thailand. And while I was curious about whether they could win, I was more interested in how they'd be received as ambassadors, not performers.

My international karaoke trips have all taken place after 9/11, and as a result, they've often reflected the current relationship between the United States and the world—or at least, the part of the world in which I happen to be singing. In early 2002, just a few months after the attacks, Kevin and I went to visit Mike in Vienna, where we were greeted warmly by other karaoke singers, some of whom gathered in big circles to sing along with us. But the following spring, as we carried on at a Barcelona karaoke bar, I looked into the audience and saw . . . no one, really. A few blocks away, demonstrators from around the country were marching on the streets, protesting the week-old war in Iraq. Even our Spanish bartender—who'd earlier performed his customized version of Lou Rawls's "You're Going to Meese My Lov-eeng"—began grilling us about President Bush. Maybe I was imagining things, but I felt like I'd gone from an object of sympathy to a likely pariah in less than a year.

In Bangkok, I hoped, I could get a read on the state of U.S.-world relations, even if the evidence was purely anecdotal. After all, if a karaoke performance is a revelation—a chance for others to "see the soul," as one of the punk-metal fans claimed—then maybe a gathering of karaoke singers from around the world would provide a glimpse of how these souls might interact if they were temporarily relieved of the burdens of politics, religion, or class. There would be a myriad of voices and languages assembling in Bangkok, and I wanted to hear them all in one place—a sort of karaoke Tower of Babel.

❧

I arrive in Thailand the night before the KWC competition is to begin, and when I check into my Bangkok hotel, I find little fanfare about the event—just a small bulletin in the lobby, informing attendees about a small meeting going on upstairs. As I ride the elevator up, I'm joined by a black man wearing sunglasses and an earring. His head is entirely shaved, save for a thin layer on the very top. I immediately recognize him as Michael Moses Griffin, one of the two American contestants.

Griffin is the most accomplished karaoke performer I've ever met: A graduate of New York's High School of Performing Arts—where he appeared as an extra in the 1980 film version of

Fame—Griffin spent three years playing with the U.S. Army Band, and he's currently working on a pair of music-related master's degrees while living outside of Chicago. In 2006, he entered (and won) his very first karaoke competition, taking home $1,000 from the Karaoke World Contest in Miami, Florida. He now travels with his own collection of karaoke backing tracks, and while en route to Bangkok, he used the layover time in Tokyo to visit a local karaoke bar just outside of the airport. "I wanted to be able to say that I sang karaoke in Japan," he tells me. Griffin appears to be in his early forties, though he won't specify his age, in part because he feels that the success of *American Idol* has unfairly stigmatized older performers. "Every application that asks 'age,' I just put 'less' next to it," he says.

After talking in the hallway for a while, Griffin and I walk to the reception area, which is suspiciously quiet. On the cruise ship, even the downtime was celebratory, and yet tonight's meeting consists of just a few dozen people sitting quietly at their tables. There's nary a whooping German to be heard; in fact, there aren't any Germans at all.

As it turns out, Germany didn't send anyone to the KWC this year. Neither did Russia, South Africa, Jordan, China, or Canada— all countries that had been represented in 2006. The most beguiling no-show is Japan, a cradle of karaoke civilization, and one that's only a seven-hour flight away. Instead, the eleven countries in attendance are once again mostly European, with contingents from Austria, Estonia, Finland, Hungary, Ireland, Poland, and Sweden. Combine them with representatives from Australia, Malaysia, Thailand, and of course the United States, and you have an international assembly that could easily be dwarfed by an after-school model-U.N. meeting, or possibly the Goodwill Games.

In the center of the room, Griffin and I take a seat at the U.S. table, where we find the other American contestant, a freckled seventeen-year-old from Dry Ridge, Kentucky, named Barbie Robbins. She has dark hair and a pierced nose, and looks a bit like a young Cameron Diaz. When Robbins was eight years old, she began singing Celine Dion songs around her home, inspiring her father to buy her a portable karaoke machine for Christmas. Since then, the two of them have made regular trips to karaoke bars near their alcohol-free hometown, so that Barbie can sneak in and practice. But her father couldn't get time off from his carpet-laying job to come here, and Barbie's mother is currently in jail for a parole violation. So the U.S. team paid to fly out her twenty-six-year-old sister, Michelle, as a chaperone. Because our hotel is located near a pair of block-wide shopping malls, the two women have already spent much of the afternoon shopping, and seem thoroughly unpumped about the meeting.

Griffin and Barbie Robbins had previously met at the American KWC finals, which were held at Cincinnati's Hamilton County Fair. The U.S. branch is still in its infancy, so the group lacked the necessary financial and organizational resources to conduct a national talent search. As a result, the regional contests were limited to Kentucky, Indiana, and Ohio. That's hardly a wide sampling of a country with 300 million people, yet I've watched enough YouTube clips of Griffin's and Robbins's performances to know they're worthy of being delegates. I only wish there was a bit more competition waiting for them here.

A few minutes before the opening speech, I hear a rumble-strip voice behind me, and I don't have to turn around to know it belongs to John Nance, one of the U.S. team's organizers. Nance is an entertainment promoter in Chicago, and we first began speaking in the summer of 2006, when he was trying to find American singers for that year's KWC event. He couldn't put a team together on time, and I knew that getting the United States a slot in the 2007 event meant a lot to him, both emotionally and financially.

Nance is a large black man in his early fifties, and the hotel attendants seem in awe of his appearance as well as his gregariousness. "Can you believe this?" he asks, patting my back with a wallop, as if to burp me. "Bangkok."

The meeting carries on for half an hour before devolving into a back-and-forth on what to do about the next few years. Nance stands up and makes a case to bring the event to his hometown of Chicago, and though I should probably stay and watch, I can't spend my first night in a new city listening to hypothetical discussions on the future of karaoke—especially when I know there's *real* karaoke awaiting me outside. So I huddle together with Griffin and the Robbins sisters and suggest we find a place to sing.

After some haggling with our Thai taxi driver—who initially wants to take us straight to a "sexy restaurant for Americans"—the four of us wind up in Patpong, a nightlife district that serves as a hub for sex-trade workers and counterfeit goods. The sidewalks are overrun by rows of brightly lit booths, and the side streets lead into shopping bazaars stacked like the Fulton Fish Market, only with cheap belt buckles and bootleg copies of *The Bourne Ultimatum* instead of mackerel. We eventually find a gay bar called the Balcony, which has a coin-operated karaoke machine and two bongos, all mercifully going unused. The cost is 10 baht (about 30 cents) for two songs, and the price includes a rather meager songlist—just a few pages of unrecognizable Thai numbers, along with some standard-issue English-language pop hits. Much to my frustration, not one of them is "One Night in Bangkok."

In the past three months, I'd become very stupidly enchanted with the idea of singing this on my trip. "One Night" was a song from the 1984 musical *Chess*, recorded by a British actor and musician named Murray Head. I had it on a 45 when I was younger, and I'm ashamed to admit that in my very early teens, it represented my sum total knowledge of Thailand. While I knew Bangkok was an Oriental city, it was mostly because the first four words of the song are "Bangkok, an Oriental city." I've since stopped using white-rap showtunes as a learning tool, yet "One Night" remains one of my favorite karaoke songs, and I assumed that residents of Bangkok would find a hometown performance to be charming. On the plane ride over, however, it occurred to me that I had no idea what "Bangkok" was actually about. What if its lyrics were in reference to some civil war or unwanted foreign annexation? Was it just coincidence that Murray Head disappeared after the song's release, or had he been abducted and flayed by a Thai mob?

Clearly, these questions will not be answered in this middling Thai gay bar, so I stare at the list for a few minutes, looking for the proper introductory song. We each take turns looking, and after a while it becomes clear that our mutual hesitancy isn't due to politeness, but awkwardness; sometimes, even the most heavily decorated karaoke singers can become flippers. Worried that we'll lose momentum, I decide to sing the Bee Gees' "Jive Talkin'," but midway through, I notice that Griffin and the Robbins sisters have left our table and are sticking their heads out the window. In the alley down below, in front of a row of cheering tourists, there's a group of tall, suspiciously broad-shouldered women sashaying down a makeshift red carpet. I've practiced my Barry Gibb impression for the last five years only to be trumped by a Thai ladyboy pageant.

Hoping to find a more open-minded song selection elsewhere, we head to a karaoke bar called the Sphinx, which is located just a few doors away. The karaoke "stage" is on the second floor above a restaurant, and it faces out toward a circular bar with earth-tone decor and lots of candles. The Sphinx's English-language selection is completely random, and, at times, spectacularly undesirable. There's a Jermaine Jackson solo track, an instrumental theme from *The Phantom Menace,* and something called "Complicated Heart" by the Danish band Michael Learns to Rock. I choose the Beatles' "Got to Get You into My Life," and a few seconds into the song, I immediately understand why professional amateurs like Griffin insist on traveling with their own karaoke discs. The "Life" lyrics are completely mistimed, and the instrumentation is brittle and faint. I give up after a minute and hand the microphone over to Griffin.

"All you people out there are beautiful, so beautiful," he says to the eight people in the bar. "I'm so glad you came tonight." He then sings "Reasons," a 1975 ballad by Earth, Wind & Fire that demonstrates Griffin's rich falsetto.

Barbie Robbins follows him, performing Christina Aguilera's "Reflections" with considerable restraint; there's not a *wooooah* of the histrionic melisma that many younger singers mistake for range, and her Kentucky accent evaporates completely. As Robbins sings, Griffin leans in and whispers that he's worried about her chances in the contest: Earlier in the day, he'd watched the other entrants sing at a sound check, and while Robbins has the best natural voice, Griffin thinks she'll be hurt by her lack of on-stage experience. "She has performance problems," he says.

After Robbins finishes, we decide to return to the hotel. The first night of the trials begins in about fifteen hours, and we could all benefit from at least that much sleep. Griffin says goodnight to a Thai couple in the back of the bar, and they promise to show up to the beer garden. "I'll be in the front row," the woman says, "yelling, 'Michael! Michael!'"

The next afternoon, I meet John Nance, the U.S. team's co-organizer, at a business lounge in our hotel, where he's wearing blue Bahama-style shorts and a gray T-shirt that says "Big Dog." "My size has a tendency to cause people to be threatened, and I don't want to threaten nobody," he tells me. "Sometimes, I really wish that I was like five foot seven and 160-something pounds. But with the same attitude."

Nance grew up in Evanston, Illinois, and was playing guitar for a string of nightclub blues-bands by the time he was fifteen. In the early '70s, he joined a funk band called Urban Crisis, and he's had several music-related jobs since, working as a DJ and a producer, and even as an inventor, creating a strobe-light device called the Disco Machine. He now helps organize cruises and live shows and hires out KJs for parties. "I work more than I talk," he says. "And I talk a lot."

In 2005, Nance received an e-mail from one of the members of the Finnish KWC team asking if he was interested in being a partner. The contract to represent the organization in the United States was up for grabs, and while Nance had little experience with running karaoke competitions, he was intrigued by the possibility of working overseas. "We're talking about the world," he says, gesturing toward the skyscrapers outside the window. "I'm in a global market." Nance tried to corral sponsors and partners for the stateside KWC only to find that the competitive-karaoke circuit was made up of hundreds of regional fiefdoms. "I spent two years reaching out to bring everybody together," he says. "There seems to be a political resistance to coming together for one cause, which I just can't understand. Don't you want a small piece of the world, rather than a big piece of Montana?"

He finally found a partner in Wendell Payne, a Cleveland-based KJ looking to break into the international karaoke market. The two men spent much of 2007 trying to get a team together for Bangkok. Although the talent-search portion of the U.S. competition wasn't as far-reaching as they'd hoped, Nance seems happy just to have made it this far. "We already accomplished what we wanted to accomplish by showing up," he says. Nance and Payne have each invested a low five-figure sum into the U.S. team, with the hopes that the KWC will eventually become a world-recognized event, much like *American Idol*. Throughout the weekend, Nance spends his time in a makeshift office in the front lobby, where he ropes in KWC attendees and outlines for them his many lucrative plans: recording deals, world tours, streaming Internet content. "At this level, it's not drunken barroom karaoke," he tells me. "You've got a bona fide performer that could be a star. Or, you have a qualified group of performers that could be stars."

I'm not sure these expectations are all that realistic. A properly maintained national talent search would require long-term planning and coordination, not to mention a lot more money. And in order to get the sort of sponsorships Nance and Payne are hoping for, they'd need for the KWC to have some sort of presence in the United States. This is why Nance wants the KWC to hold its finals in Chicago within the next two years. If they can get enough press and industry attention from the event, he reasons, it could give the organization more credibility within the United States.

"I'm trying to get them to realize that if you really want to be a major player, you gotta do the U.S.," he says. "I'm in their face all the time. I made it known to the whole entire group last night: If you come to Chicago, you won't have any of this stupid bullshit here." Nance's voice rises in agitation. He's frustrated by the low turnout this year and worries it will dissuade the KWC from holding the event in other countries. Before I left for Bangkok, the group had announced plans to hold the 2008 contest in Beijing, just in time for the Olympics; now, there are rumors that it may not leave Finland at all. If that's the case, Nance thinks the group will lose the opportunity to cultivate a truly international audience. "If you want to be a world-class organization, you've got to have a world-class point of view," he says. "If it's in Antarctica, we'll get our parkas, we'll get our dogs, and we'll mush their behinds to the South Pole. If it's in outer space, put our people in that rocketship. We'll get on there. As a matter of fact, we'll take the rocketship *first.*"

He leans back and assumes a questionably humble shrug. "I'm into this for the *deal,*" he says. "And if it provides me with a life, then that will be my just reward."

Nance is right: There has been some stupid bullshit here, though it's hard to place the blame squarely on the KWC organization. Most of the planning was coordinated by a pair of Thai businessmen, both of whom had lobbied extensively for years to bring the event to Bangkok. But just a few months before the contest, the two men had a falling-out and pulled out of the competition. When the Finnish KWC team arrived here to salvage the contest, they found that the original venue would only hold a few hundred people. So yes, mistakes were made. But to the organizers' credit, they managed to find the Suan-Lun Night Bazaar, a six-year-old outdoor beer garden that was seemingly built for the express purpose of hosting an international karaoke contest.

The Bazaar is set up like a small football arena, with the audience members on the field, food vendors on the sideline, and an elevated stage as one of the end zones. There's no charge for admission, and the audience is mostly young locals in their teens and twenties—just the sort of people who are apt to spend their weekend nights eating crab salads, drinking from elaborate beer taps, and watching whatever free entertainment is plopped in front of them for a good three to four hours.

Upon arriving on the first night of trials, I find that the KWC groups have segregated themselves by country: Swedes, Hungarians, and Poles to the left, Irish and Australians to the right (not surprisingly, the right side is the loudest throughout most of the night). The Austrian karaoke team is the easiest to spot, as its members are all wearing red T-shirts proclaiming "AUSTRIAN KARAOKE TEAM." I make my way to the Americans, who are sitting directly in front of the loudspeakers, which means that we have to shout to make ourselves heard above Aerosmith's insufferable "Don't Want to Miss a Thing," which plays every time there's an intermission.

By the stage, Griffin is drinking a screwdriver and chatting up some Swedes. "This place is like a bar," he says. "I always feel good in a bar." I ask if he's at all nervous, and he turns around and looks at the audience members who are gathering around the tables behind him. "I'm more anxious than nervous," he says. "I wanna sing. These are my people."

Barbie Robbins, meanwhile, is trying to get her cell phone to call some friends back home. This trip came together for her in just a matter of weeks; she seems relaxed, but I suspect that she hasn't entirely processed the fact that she's here in Bangkok. The KWC contestants are allowed to choose their own songs, and Griffin has carefully calibrated his setlist. Robbins, however, didn't do much planning with her running order. In a karaoke competition, this qualifies as a grave tactical error: The KWC permits each singer to select five songs, the first three of which will be performed before the eliminations begin. After his win in Miami last year, Griffin knows how to strategize. He'll open with Earth, Wind

& Fire's "September," which allows him to dance and interact with the crowd, and he'll follow that with Prince's "Purple Rain," as ballads are usually a better showcase of vocal range.

Robbins didn't factor in these considerations, and though she selected karaoke mainstays such as "I Will Always Love You" and "Son of a Preacher Man," she essentially handed over her disc with a shrug. Since it's too late for her to amend her song selection, we sit at the unofficial American table, watching the show unfold. It begins with the previous year's winner singing "My Heart Will Go On"—the karaoke-contest equivalent of not merely gilding the lily, but drenching that lily with Pier One body butter, strapping it to a rocket, and using it to blow up the sun. Once the song is through, the contestants begin their performances.

Juha Karvonen (Finland)

Looking a bit like Patrick Swayze, but in black leather pants, Karvonen sings a power ballad that I can't identify, though he later tells the emcee his favorite band is Whitesnake, which may be a clue. "The singer, David Coverdale?" he says to the crowd. "From him I learned a lot."

Barbie Robbins (U.S.A.)

Though her voice is assured, Robbins hardly moves at all, singing "I Will Always Love You" while seemingly cooped up in an invisible one-foot fence.

Marcello Maturana (Sweden)

While performing Radiohead's "Creep," Maturana wears black eyeliner, a loosened tie, and an untucked shirt. During the "float like a feather" lyric, he points out to the crowd and slowly drops his hand, and sings the last part of his song while on his knees.

Gabriella Lukacs (Hungary)

Singing AC/DC's "Highway to Hell" while clad in black shorts and a billowy white shirt, Lukacs' performance is frequently drowned out by Nance, who's drinking a Long Island Iced Tea the size of Massapequa and yelling "Hot pants! Hot pants! Hot pants! Yeah!" though she is not technically wearing hot pants.

Michael Moses Griffin (U.S.A.)

"What month is this?" Griffin asks as the song begins. "Is it . . . *September?*" Griffin then executes a series of well-rehearsed dance moves, including the Traffic Stop (swiveling his neck left and right between verses) and the Eva Perón Roof-Raise (stretching his arm out with the palm facing up).

When Robbins emerges from backstage after her performance, Griffin runs up and gives her a hug. She holds out her hands. "I'm shaking," she says.

In the second round, Griffin performs "Purple Rain," which is even more theatrical than "September," as his jacket comes off halfway through the song. Only two songs into the competition, he's an early favorite, and by the end of "Rain," a knot of audience members rush to the front, singing along and swaying their arms.

Unfortunately, I miss Barbie's second number, though not without good reason. Near the entrance of the beer garden is a series of private karaoke stalls, which are lined up in rows and look to be only slightly roomier than a standard-issue American phone booth. In a small enclosure nearby, I see a fiftysomething man wearing sandals and glasses, and working on a sketch of a robot; he introduces himself as Mr. Pornchai and invites me into his workspace. Mr. Pornchai is an inventor, and a few years ago, he created a special type of CD-changer, which led him to the karaoke business. He's now the secretary of Thai Karaoke Configuration, a consortium of karaoke-industry employees. According to Mr. Pornchai, karaoke only took off in Thailand about ten years ago, and his booths now draw about 100 visitors a day: Older patrons sing folk songs, while young customers favor hip-hop and Thai swing music.

The rest of our conversation is mired by my rudimentary Thai-language skills, but if I hear him correctly, one of Mr. Pornchai's favorite karaoke artists is the Scorpions. Either that, or he was trying to warn me about the threat of *actual* scorpions. It's a tricky lingo.

I walk into one of the stalls and look for "One Night in Bangkok," only to find that the track selection consists mostly of Thai hip-hop and glossy Eastern European ballads. After finally locating a disc of English-language songs, I put in my coins and choose an old Chicago song. But the machine begins to sputter and skip, and so while Barbie's on stage, I'm blindly punching at a row of buttons, to no avail. Ten minutes later, I walk by the booth once again, where I can hear Peter Cetera's voice repeating on a loop, as if to taunt me: "If you leave me now . . . if you leave me now . . . if you leave me now . . ."

The first night of competition finally ends after midnight, with eliminations scheduled to begin tomorrow. An ad hoc international summit is held by the tuk-tuk line, where it's decided that, after four straight hours of karaoke, what we all really need is a karaoke bar. The only problem is that nobody knows where to go: The KWC group hasn't coordinated any post-show parties or events, leaving the contestants to fend for themselves. This led to an unfortunate incident the night before, when several Swedes asked to be driven to a karaoke bar and instead were taken to a go-go club where the bartenders charged 300 baht ($9) per beer, and where nobody was allowed to sing. "If you see 'MASSAGE' in neon," one of the Swedes tells me, "it's not a good sign."

Eventually, about twenty people wind up back in the lobby of our hotel, which is where we remain for the rest of the night, as it's completely vacated and within a one-minute walk of a late-night beer distributor. There's a piano in the corner, and Mattias Cederlund, one of the cosponsors for the Swedish team, begins playing "Stand by Me," luring several contestants to form a circle around him and sing along. In Sweden, Cederlund produces karaoke tracks and ringtones, but he played in a few bands when he was younger, which might explain why he has a seemingly endless recall of every song request that comes his way, from "My Way" to "Isn't She Lovely" to "Sweet Child O'Mine." When the group gathers to sing "Carrie," the 1986 ballad by the heavy-metal band Europe, some of the hotel staffers circle the piano, as though they want to join in, only to quietly retreat.

A few feet away, Barbie Robbins sits at a rowdy lobby table, where the beer cans already have grip marks, and the conversation has turned to the war in Iraq. World affairs is not a strong subject for Barbie, who'd never even been on a plane until this week. She seems genuinely taken aback when she's told that some countries don't like the United States, and this reaction draws a few condescending asides around the table. But instead of wilting away, Robbins asks questions of her captors, as though engaging in a geopolitical debate with drunken Scandinavians in Southeast Asia is a common Friday-night rite. Throughout the weekend, as various international disputes are outlined for her, Robbins often responds by widening her eyes and saying, "But people are people." She repeats this as if it were a simple code, one the rest of the world simply refuses to decipher.

I'm slightly in awe of Barbie, who's seventeen years old and the least traveled person here, and yet seems more open-minded and assured than some of the adults. When the contest is over, she'll head back to her Kentucky hometown for her senior year of high school, where she'll have to decide whether she wants to pursue a career in music. Barbie has natural musical talent, but it's underfed and unrefined. She can't read sheet music, doesn't know what to do on an open stage, and aside from her time in Bangkok, her performance career consists of a few failed *American Idol* tryouts, some underage karaoke-bar gigs, and a three-week music camp. She needs a proper musical education, one that she probably won't be able to find in Dry Ridge. "It's really like a hillbilly town," she says. "A little town in such a big world."

Still, Robbins isn't sure whether leaving Dry Ridge is worth the risk, as she wouldn't be able to spend much time with her boyfriend or their three-month-old son. She's considering applying to the music program at the University of Cincinnati, or maybe staying at home and studying nursing. And though she plans on trying out for *Idol* again, she knows that if she doesn't make it, her music-business opportunities are limited to whatever she can find at home. "It's kind of a big conflict," she sighs. "If I got a music scholarship, I'd go anywhere. I'd probably even come back *here*. I'd do anything for music."

All international competitions tend to encourage nationalist pride and hyperbole, and the KWC is no exception. Perhaps because karaoke was so widely looked down upon for years, some of the attendees feel compelled to pull me aside and remind me that they live in the Greatest Karaoke Country in the World. *It's in every bar!* they say, no matter where they're from. *Every house! We got it right after the Japanese!* I'd seen such behavior on the Helsinki cruise, where a Finnish man semi-belligerently insisted that Helsinki had more karaoke bars per capita than all of Japan, an absolutely bonkers statement, yet one I couldn't disprove with statistics.

Knowing I'd be harangued in Bangkok with fantastical, unverifiable tales of karaoke superiority, I consulted Roger Kurobe before going to Thailand. In the early '80s, Kurobe worked as the overseas sales chief for Kay Takagi, the Japanese entrepreneur who imported the Singing Machine to America. Kurobe's job required him to travel from one country to the next, introducing karaoke machines to new markets. This makes him a leading authority on karaoke world history, and I wish I could have brought him with me to Bangkok, just so I could have an on-the-spot conversational expert, like Marshall McLuhan in *Annie Hall.*

According to Kurobe, there were several cultural obstacles involved in getting those early 8-track karaoke machines out of Japan and into the rest of the world. His first job was as an exporter to Taiwan, where the government had strict customs regulations, which forced Kurobe to smuggle in the machines himself. Three times a week, he'd fly from Japan to Taiwan with a karaoke machine in his luggage, and when he arrived, he'd go straight to a predetermined declaration table, where an insider would wave him through. After that, he moved on to Singapore, which was equally problematic, though for different reasons: Members of several musicians' unions were afraid of losing their patrons to karaoke and had successfully lobbied the government to ban all machines. The prohibition lasted for two years, until Kurobe finally convinced the unions that his machines wouldn't destroy their businesses. Everywhere Kurobe went, he had to overcome some unique local barriers, all of which required research and diplomacy. In India, he found that while Bollywood films encouraged people to sing, many Indians didn't want to drink in public. So Kurobe focused on portable, at-home machines. In Germany, meanwhile, he discovered that some people didn't believe they *needed* a singing machine, as they'd already been singing in beer gardens and beer halls for years. He had a similar problem in Italy, thanks in part, he says, to the country's operatic traditions. Just about every country eventually relented, except for France. "Very difficult country," Kurobe sighs. "They have very high pride."

As Kurobe continued to travel, he began to realize that the biggest impediment to karaoke's success was its reputation as a boozy, vice-spurring activity. So he began meeting with educators, trying to convince them that the machines could be used to teach English. "I tried to make karaoke a very healthy activity," he says. This approach helped him break into Africa and northern Europe, and it's what brought him to America in 1985. While living in California—and occasionally taking business trips to Nashville, where he rented a house from Willie Nelson—Kurobe partnered with literacy groups, espousing karaoke as a way to teach reading. He also claims to have introduced karaoke machines to a prison in Atlanta, where they were used to ease relations between African-American and Hispanic inmates. The program's success resulted in a letter of gratitude from President Bill Clinton. "That's how I got my green card," Kurobe says.

Kurobe took his karaoke machines to more than forty countries between 1983 and 2001—which may be why so many people I meet at the KWC are convinced that their home is the one true karaoke motherland. He now licenses cartoon characters in Japan, but after watching karaoke become more popular over the past few years, he's thinking about getting back into the business. One of Kurobe's strongest markets in the '80s was Latin America, and with the growing Latino population, he envisions specialized k-boxes, where Spanish-language customers can walk in, sing a song, and get a recording of their performances. "One song per dollar," Kurobe says. "I want to install one in every shopping mall."

On the second night of competition, I spend an hour standing near the back of the Suan-Lun Night Bazaar, trying to get a sense of the audience's size. The KWC claims the venue holds 10,000 visitors over the course of two nights, though there are so many people coming and going that it's impossible to get an accurate head count; over the course of the weekend, I never see it at full capacity. As I watch a bald, slightly rotund Irish man singing "Mr. Bojangles" on a stage adorned by two giant beer barrels, I can only guess what the stragglers must be thinking as they file into the garden. From back here, it looks like a jukebox-musical based on the life of Donkey Kong.

Booking the beer garden may have been a lucky break for the KWC managers, but it was one of few they'd get this year. The group recruits many foreign partners from the Internet, with each country responsible for organizing its own local trials. Countries pay 1,500 euros each for the partnership, some of which goes toward the prize money (the 2007 pot totals about 5,500 euros, which is just over $8,000). But even with those funds, the KWC can't afford to send members to each country to supervise, and the team has to place a lot of trust in people they've never met. Like all Internet courtships, this occasionally ends in heartbreak.

According to organizers, many of the countries that bailed on this year's contest did so for financial reasons, citing the high costs of traveling to Bangkok. This makes some sense, as certainly, it's much cheaper for northern Europeans to go to Finland than it is for them to fly to Thailand. But the poor turnout couldn't have come at a worse time for the KWC, as this was intended as a bit of an international coming-out party. Nance isn't the only one who thinks the event has *Idol*-like potential, and the organizers want the KWC to become an international brand, with big-name sponsorships and a global audience. But when the group's Bangkok sponsors pulled out unexpectedly, it forced KWC's organizers to reconsider their globalization strategy. By the second night, it's official: In 2008, the contest will remain safely ensconced in Finland, much to the chagrin of John Nance.

Few of the contestants seem to be aware of any of the behind-the-scenes politics, and I doubt they'd even care, as so many of them have already settled into full-time careers. They are construction workers, IT consultants, and operations managers, and while they certainly wouldn't refuse a chance to sing professionally, no one seems to think that a first-place win will somehow grant them automatic fame.

This may explain why the alleyway near the entrance has turned into a congenial greenroom, where participants hang out to share cigarettes and praise. It's here that I find Marcello Maturana, the Swede who had put on the performance of Radiohead's "Creep" the night before. While waiting for his turn to go on, he's palling around with one of the Irish competitors. He doesn't seem particularly anxious about the contest. "For me, it's a vacation more than a singing competition," he says. Maturana is twenty-five, and he only became aware of his voice in his late teens, while singing along with a car radio. "I thought, 'I'm hitting every note,'" he says. "So I sing for a little while, and then pick up the guitar. I'm a rocker. I love grunge."

Maturana also loves Creed, the stroke-mouthed guitar-rock group I once believed to be the worst band in America, only to realize it's actually the worst band in the world. After we talk, he sings the band's 2001 power ballad "My Sacrifice." The song is just as awful as I remember, but Maturana's performance is actually quite moving: He casts his gaze skyward, as though a spaceship were about to swoop down and pick him up, and whirls his microphone around with zeal. I can't understand his connection to the song, but at least I can see it. Even if I can't entirely relate, karaoke gives me an entry point.

Once Maturana is finished, there are just a few more performances before the cuts are announced.

Kelvin Lu Hee Wah (Malaysia)

A jewelry salesman who's lived in Bangkok for the past few years, Kelvin brings a stool onto the stage and dedicates his song "to all my Thai friends." "I might or might not get to see you again," he says. "This song reminds me of when I was dumped nine years ago. It's a song about hope." He then sings a Thai-language ballad, drawing emphatic cheers from the crowd.

Barbie Robbins (U.S.A.)

Wearing a purple T-shirt and jeans, Barbie sings Dusty Springfield's "Son of a Preacher Man." After omitting a few lines—and coming in way too early on a few others—she all but freezes up onstage.

A Drunk Hungarian Guy Singing Starship's "We Built This City" (Hungary)

Wow.

Vanessa Cooney (Ireland)

Not long after Barbie's performance, Vanessa also sings "Son of a Preacher Man," never missing a note or a single lyric. Even before Cooney gets to the chorus, it's clear that Barbie is doomed.

Barbie's rendition of "Preacher Man" was excruciating to watch: The song all but escaped her grasp within the first minute, and you could tell she knew it. Afterward, she says the track she gave the sound technician wasn't a CD+G file, but an MP3, meaning there weren't any lyrics for her to follow on-screen. When her name isn't called among the five female finalists, she's neither sad nor surprised. When Griffin's name is announced as one of the five male finalists, he and Barbie high-five and hug.

As the final rounds commence, it becomes clear that Griffin has stored his most dramatic numbers for the end, as though he were a funk tantric. Halfway through a version of Rick James's "Give It to Me," the buttons at the top and bottom of his shirt suddenly go off duty, and he moves around so much that his pants fill up like windsocks. "If you're not dancing," he tells the crowd, "there's something wrong with your butt."

Griffin has more on-stage experience than any of the other KWC participants, as his singing career began when he was six years old. His mother was an opera singer, and his father toured with a gospel group. Griffin was often recruited to sing in church. "I had music everywhere," he says. "I've always been singing in some capacity, even if it was just to myself." He grew up in nearly every borough of New York City, and left the North Bronx when he was eighteen to study at Shenandoah Conservatory of Music, the first stop in a still-ongoing music-education tour. When he completes his master's degrees, he plans to go into teaching, which may be why he speaks in prescriptive terms when discussing Barbie. "I think if I had had a month to work with her, it would have been a totally different outcome," he says after her performance. "I would have told her flat out, 'You must know every single word cold. Even if you trip, and fall on your head on stage, the words should still be coming out of your mouth.'"

By the time Griffin and the other finalists complete their last performances, it's stretching close to midnight, and the hot air is mixing with the smell of trash. There's an ugly, cranky feral cat wandering the grounds, and as we're waiting for the judges to return, he brushes by my leg and hisses at me. After two days, even he's fed up with all the Diane Warren ballads.

Finally, the judges are called back to their seats, and a swarm of dramatic-looking spotlights—each one bearing an illustration of an old-timey microphone—start flashing the beer garden. As the ten finalists line up on stage, they try to resist the urge to look too serious, which only makes their anxiousness more apparent. Griffin winds up taking second place in the men's division, with first place going to Kelvin, the Malaysian singer. The women's division, meanwhile, awards first prize to Julie Walter-Sgro, an Australian singer. Vanessa Cooney, the Irish singer whose "Son of a Preacher Man" rendition likely helped knock Barbie out of the running, comes in second place. Amazingly, the drunken Hungarian places fifth.

All of the contestants are then brought back out on stage to sing one last song: "We Are the World," which also closed out the 2006 competition. It's an obvious choice, but really, it's not as if anyone else has recorded a halfway decent world-harmony hit in the past twenty-five years. When the song ends, a little girl walks on stage, and somebody begins an a cappella version of "We Are the Champions." There are no verses—just the title chorus over and over again as the little girl waves to the crowd. Flags from nearly every country cut the air.

And though it's all irredeemably hokey, I take this all in, and I start to think, *Hey, maybe we* are *the world—and maybe even the champions, too!*

I'm conscious of how stupid that sounds, and how foolish it would be to treat this scene as a microcosm of the world at large (especially since so much of the world isn't even represented). Having a few shared cultural references isn't the same thing as having a shared culture, and just because everyone here knows the words to an old song about peace, it doesn't mean they wouldn't eventually blow each other's legs off over an oil reserve in Kabul.

But maybe it does.

Here's what both of these trips have proved to me: We don't know anything about anyone. Granted, we've gathered plenty of intelligence on each other's cultures and history and behavior, but those aren't actually *truths;* they're just facts. And for me, karaoke is most rewarding when it proves those facts wrong. Whatever perceptions I have about people—no matter where they're from— are usually debunked as soon as they open their mouths, and that's a humbling feeling. I leave the beer garden feeling the same way I did when I left that Pennsylvania sports bar almost a decade earlier, wondering how many things I'd always been wrong about.

♪

The closing-night after-party is once again held in the hotel lobby. Word must have spread about Cederlund, the piano-playing Swede, as there are nearly a dozen people plying him with requests, including "Great Balls of Fire," "Bridge over Troubled Water," and "Imagine," for which everyone stops and sings. When I tell Cederlund about my inability to find "One Night in Bangkok," he begins playing a few bars, noting, with no shortage of Scandinavian pride, that the song was written by the two guys from ABBA. I quietly take a few turns at the chorus and then turn the piano stool back to the real singers.

There are only two hotel attendants on duty, and for the next few hours, they barely look at us—not even when a Finnish metalhead starts screaming by the outside entrance, or when the Polish guy starts screaming at me about his love for Diana Krall. At 5:58 A.M., we all line up by the restaurant, waiting for the complimentary breakfast to begin. As soon as the doors open, we fill our plates high with shitty sausages, and they are, without a doubt, the best shitty sausages any of us have ever had.

The Swedes and I take a table in the back, where we can watch from a safe distance, as we're a bit more sober than the rest of the group. At one point, Cederlund casually points his fork toward the front of the restaurant. "The Polish guy is singing in the buffet," he says.

I turn around and see the Polish guy standing near the breakfast line, crooning as he fills his plate. The other customers clutch their dishes close and stare at him with sympathetic concern, the way you would at an old lady who walks into the middle of traffic. There are a few early-rise businessmen sitting around us, and one of them folds down his newspaper and stares at our table disapprovingly, as though *we* were the ones who told the guy to start singing to the waffles.

I start thinking that this might be a good time to leave.

There's a pool upstairs, and though it's not scheduled to open for another forty-five minutes, the Finnish metalhead swears it's unlocked. We all break off to go back to our rooms, planning to re-convene on the pool deck. Apparently, we lose some of our fellow travelers along the way, because only a small group makes it intact: four Americans, two Finns, and three Swedes (including Matu-rana, who apparently didn't bring a bathing suit, and who simply walks into the pool still wearing his clothes from the night before). There's a contingent of senior Chinese ladies doing their morning laps, but they're not supposed to be in the pool, either, and there-fore can't complain to the management. They withdraw to the hot tub, bobbing their swimcaps in silent defeat. The pool is ours.

I do a cannonball, even though the signs warn against jumping or diving. The water is warm from the rising sun, and I make a calm descent to the bottom, where I feel the grate with my fingers and listen to the other bodies plunging around me. When I come back up for air, the Finnish metalhead is sitting on a lounge chair, singing Dio's "Holy Diver." It's 7 A.M. on a Sunday morning in Bangkok, and he's trying to figure out where he can find more beer.

I get out and find a towel, and see Griffin on the edge of the pa-tio. "This is perfect," I say to him. "This is how the world should be."

"Yeah," he says. "But it could never happen."

"Why not?" I ask.

"People are people," he says.

CHAPTER 10

Abe Lincoln Sings

Honolulu, Hawaii

I've only been back to my old neighborhood for an hour, and already, I'm stupid with nostalgia. Every time I pass by some old building or landmark—even the ones with dubious personal significance—I become undeservedly wistful. "Hey, look," I think. "It's that old bus shelter. I *know* I waited for the bus there one time. Crazy!" Then I pull over and take a picture.

I'll never understand why I'm like this. I suppose it could be a natural consequence of aging, but I'm only in my thirties, and the onset of crazy-talk isn't supposed to begin until I'm at least forty or so. Or it could just be a way to silence the low-level dread that's nowadays always in the background, humming like a decrepit fluorescent that no one knows how to fix. But I'm guessing that reminiscence is really just an act of reassurance: I was alive then, and I'm alive now, so the odds are pretty good that I can keep this all going for a while.

I hadn't actually planned on coming back to Hawaii, but a friend of mine was out here for work and offered to let me crash in his hotel room for a few days. Unfortunately, on the night before I flew out, I decided to go to a Los Angeles karaoke bar called Caffe Brass Monkey, where I surpassed the two-drink minimum and sang a notably self-assured version of Harvey Danger's late-'90s hit "Flagpole Sitta." As soon as I finished, one of the bar patrons handed me a paper plate with a large slice of birthday cake, and here in Hawaii, I'm still feeling the combined effects of Duncan Heinz, whiskey, and regret. I'm not sick, but I'm not well.

One of the reasons I've come here is to find the karaoke bar that my father went to back in the late '80s, the place where he sang "New York, New York," thus initiating my fascination with karaoke. But first, I want to pay a visit to my old junior-high school and take a stroll around the campus. When I drive into the school's parking lot, though, a security guard immediately begins walking toward my car. It's a Saturday afternoon, but there are kids practicing soccer outside, and I realize that a thirtysomething guy with a hangover and no reason to be here might look a bit suspect. I don't want an uncomfortable conversation to ruin my happily nostalgic mood, so I drive off, a bit stung by my old school's modern-day safety measures, and saddened by the fact that they're probably necessary.

I've set aside the rest of the day to find that old karaoke bar, so I call my father to see if he can give me at least an idea of where it might be located. Alas, his navigational skills are lacking, and if his directions had been computed by MapQuest, they'd look something like this:

1. Start out going SOUTHEAST toward THAT ONE BIG ROAD THAT GOES TO THE BIG MALL (0.4 miles).

2. Continue on WHATEVER THAT ROAD IS CALLED until you get to WHEREVER THE OLD TOWER RECORDS USED TO BE (0.1 miles).
3. Look for a small SHOPPING AREA OF SOME SORT, maybe one with a PARKING LOT? (-2.3 miles).
4. Hold on, I'm going to ASK YOUR MOTHER.

I drive around this vaguely defined perimeter for an hour and a half, pulling into every tiny shopping area that I can find. There's one karaoke bar that fits my father's description, but when I talk to the guy working behind the counter, he tells me it's only been open for a few years. At one point, I see a beaten-up sign in my rearview mirror, and it's only after making an illegal four-lane U-turn that I realize it actually reads KARATE.

This is getting sad.

I only have a few days in Hawaii, and I'm wasting them by going from one ugly strip mall to the next, in search of a place that probably hasn't been open in ten years. And for what? It's just a karaoke bar, and at this point, I've seen enough karaoke bars to know exactly what to expect. As much as I'd like to find this place—to fill in the one missing piece of my karaoke history—I should be sleeping at the beach, or at the very least, spray-painting murals of Don Ho, whose recent death is being mourned with Tupac-like reverence.

I fold up my maps and start driving back to the hotel. When I pull to an intersection stop, I notice a small backstreet, one that I'd somehow overlooked, even though I'd covered this whole neighborhood twice already. As soon as I turn the corner, I see a cramped storefront with the word KARAOKE above it. The tinted black windows are now brown from sun and age, and when I step out of the car and look around, I can see a sign across the street for the now-defunct Tower Records.

This has to be the place, I think. It's exactly where my father said it would be, and the only way it could look more '80s would be if Lee Iacocca was out front, posing for a Nagel portrait. I try to open the door, but it's locked, even though the hours listed on the front indicate that it should be open by now. No one responds when I knock, so I just move my forehead back and forth across the window like a squeegee, looking for any clues. All I can see are stacks of cardboard moving boxes, which I imagine are full of the most wondrous collection of karaoke laser-discs ever assembled. Clearly, this place had been dead for weeks, if not months. I'd come all the way here to find it, only to be separated by a few inches.

Shit.

I swing around and notice *another* karaoke bar across the street, this one bright and sterile. There are a few employees at the door, and I'm guessing they'll know where I can find whoever owns this place. If I can track down the manager, maybe I can get inside and take a look around. But just as I'm about to walk over and ask, I start thinking: What's the point?

I've imagined what this bar looked like since I was twelve years old. It's where all of my karaoke adventures inadvertently began, and it represents a brief, ephemeral overlap between my father's life and my own. But if I walk inside, all the images I've had in my head will be contradicted, and eventually erased. I don't want that to happen, as I'm perfectly happy with the way I imagine it now: small tables, bickering customers, and my dad in the middle of it all, singing Sinatra for one night only. I may be overly sentimental of the past, but if I keep trying to re-create it, there'll be nothing left to reminisce about. After a while, I'll be left with merely nostalgia for nostalgia.

So I get back in my car and drive away. I want to see if my favorite gas station is still around, and after that, there's an old water fountain I want to say hi to.

The next afternoon, I drive out to another local school, one that's a bit more hospitable than my own. President William McKinley High is located in the city's downtown area, where it sits next to high palm trees and a bronze statue of its namesake president, a leading proponent of Hawaiian statehood. On the front steps of the school's auditorium, I find a group of women dressed in muumuus and carrying flowers. One of them hands me a canary-yellow program with an illustration of a cocksure tiger holding a microphone. Underneath, it reads:

> McKinley Alumni Association
> Sixth Annual Karaoke Challenge
> April 29, 2007
> 1:00 p.m.

There are more than thirty-five singers listed in the program, most of them graduates from the '50s and '60s. One of the women working the front door tells me all of the singers are amateurs, and many of them will be performing in costume. She also tells me the show is scheduled to run for two hours. Not surprisingly, tickets are still available.

I take a moment to acknowledge the fortuitous timing of my Hawaii trip and then make my $20 donation. There are about 800 people in the auditorium, primarily Asian-Americans who graduated around the same time as the performers; as far as I can tell, I'm the only thirtysomething haole in attendance. I take a seat in the back row, and just as the lights dim, a woman in front of me turns around, smiles sweetly, and says, "Now what brings *you* here?"

I tell her it's a long story.

The curtain opens to reveal a white wooden gate in center stage, with a collection of international flags hanging overhead. The singers are introduced one by one as they walk through the gate, taking a moment to bow for the audience. Not all of them are McKinley graduates: As the emcee explains, the school leaves a few slots open for novice singers from within the community who were recruited and trained by karaoke *sensei*. I've never heard such a term, and it immediately makes me think of a dojo filled with stern-faced men in robes, barking out Survivor songs. But it's actually a well-known occupation in Japan, where people hire a karaoke *sensei* to help them perfect a song, which might then be performed in front of friends or coworkers. Here at McKinley, the *sensei* are treated like V.I.P.s. They're even sitting in reserved seats near the front of the auditorium.

This afternoon's show is emceed by an older gentleman named Edwin, and he opens with a zinger. "It's a daytime event this year," he tells the crowd, "because some people were so old, they couldn't drive home at night." It gets a laugh, though as one of the organizers tells me later, it's actually true. The Karaoke Challenge was started in 2002 by several members of the class of 1957, who were trying to find a more efficient fundraiser for the school. Because karaoke has long been popular in Honolulu—it was introduced by Japanese businessmen in the '80s, and embraced by anecdote-needy tourists in the early '90s—the school decided to hold a yearly karaoke competition. This year, though, organizers wanted to make the event more accessible to non-alumni, which is why they brought in the *sensei*, rolled back the start time, and turned the challenge into a talent show rather than a contest.

Still, it takes nearly fifteen minutes of introductions before the arrival of the first performer, a 1968 graduate who sings Billy Ray Cyrus's "Achy Breaky Heart" while dressed in a cowboy hat and accompanied by twelve line dancers (dubbed the "Electric Slide Dancers" in the program). It's an audacious opening, one that sets the tone for the nearly twenty numbers that follow: There's a heavily sequined performance of "Papa Loves Mambo"; a version of the '30s ballad "Darling, Je Vous Aime Beaucoup," in which the singer performs for a miniature white dog and a group of bopping cardboard trees; and a rendition of the Mamas and the Papas' "California Dreamin'," featuring hippie wigs and tambourines. There are also a few traditional Hawaiian songs, and a *mahalo* (or "thank you") number that consists of a very dramatic rendition of "Born Free."

For the final performance, an Asian gentleman in his fifties walks onto the stage, wearing a business suit adorned with a lei and a medal. He's introduced as Richard Sakoda, the chairman of the event's steering committee and a former karaoke contest winner. In 1991, Sakoda took first place in a local contest sponsored by a Japanese radio station, whose staff then sent him to Tokyo to compete in an international championship. He didn't win, but when he returned, he started promoting karaoke contests around Honolulu. Sakoda now helps the school with its annual fundraiser, which he's hoping to expand in coming years. "We're thinking of doing one-on-one shows with the other high schools," he tells me after the McKinley performance. "But no one's really at the point we are yet."

As the leader of the Karaoke Challenge committee, it falls upon Sakoda to perform the event's closing number. As he walks out to the front of the stage and takes a bow, the piano introduction to John Lennon's "Imagine" plunks over the sound system. Sakoda begins singing about heaven and hell, and soon the show's other performers file on stage behind him. Some are dressed in costumes that were clearly being saved for closing-number gravitas: One man is clad as a Polynesian warrior, while another is a simple hobo. There are entire countries represented by headwear, including a beret and a mariachi hat.

And then, out of nowhere, Abraham Lincoln shows up in the back row, next to a very grave-looking Mary Todd Lincoln, his very own Yoko. Mr. Lincoln remains perfectly still as he performs, which not only lends him an appropriately stately air, but also probably helps keep his beard attached. And he doesn't move until the end, when all the performers raise their index fingers to the sky to invoke the song's hopeful end-note: Someday, the world will live as one.

As they finish, I look over my shoulder, just in case a singing John Wilkes Booth tries to rush the stage and ruin the mood.

The "Imagine" production is like a modestly budgeted fever dream, and as I watch it, I realize that I didn't come to Hawaii to relive my past. I came here to see my future. Even from my seat in the back row, I can look behind all the props and hats and slain-president costumes and recognize the joy that karaoke gives these people. It's the same joy I get on an early weekend night, when the karaoke room is only just starting to fill up, and the song I've been waiting to hear all day begins to play on those raspy, archaic speakers. For those of us who love karaoke, that's the moment in which we can silence all of our other fears and doubts, even if only temporarily. And it's that moment which unites us, no matter what we choose to sing. Fifty years from now, I'll be doing exactly what these McKinley graduates are doing here today: Standing in a room with a bunch of pals, singing karaoke songs, and not caring about how I look or sound.

As the McKinley audience stands to applaud, the emcee leads them in the school's fight song. I don't know the words, but I sing along anyway.

Adventures
in
Karaoke

Frank Sinatra, "New York, New York"
August 18, 2007
Burlington, Vermont

The best karaoke session of my life lasted only forty-five minutes, cost a few hundred dollars, and featured a tiny songlist that did not include "Sister Christian." Yet I still tipped. It was that good.

I'd performed karaoke at a wedding only once before, in 2006, when my childhood friend Kevin got married in Sioux Falls, South Dakota; he'd met the bride through a mutual friend, and proceeded to woo her over several months at a few karaoke sessions. Mike and I were groomsmen, and Kevin hired a DJ whose playlist included a few karaoke songs. As grateful as I was for this decision, I became concerned about the DJ's musical instincts as the evening went on: When he found out that Kevin was from the Philadelphia suburbs, he played Bruce Springsteen's "Streets of

Philadelphia," which, though technically a slow song, is a slow song about AIDS.

The DJ had a narrow karaoke-song selection, but after some deliberations on what would be the most appropriate wedding song, the three of us took to the dance floor to perform Starship's "We Built This City," which I'm sure the DJ normally saved for Masons meetings. We performed it in our typically overaggressive manner, and though there were a few hundred people there, it felt like we were back at Village Karaoke, once again throwing our own private party. Jenny watched from our table, her hands occasionally covering her eyes. She'd long ago learned to accept and/or ignore such asininity. We got engaged a few months later.

When the time came for us to plan our own wedding, I exhaustively researched the karaoke scene in northern Vermont, a task that took all of twenty seconds. I found a DJ who promised to reserve the last forty-five minutes of the reception for karaoke, which was a bit of a risk. While I knew a few of my friends would be willing to sing, I wasn't sure just how many uncles and cousins would share our karaoke fervor, and I didn't want to pay an extra $400 for a karaoke machine that would go unused. Plus, I wasn't sure if my regular karaoke numbers were appropriate for a pair of newlyweds. At Kevin's wedding, the Starship selection had made sense: "We Built This City" may be a goof, but at least it espouses the virtues of a strong foundation, however indirectly. Somehow, I doubted a song like "On Our Own" could be quite as meaningful, and I wasn't sure if imitating Bobby Brown was a fitting way to celebrate a marriage.

When I showed up at the reception and saw our track selection, though, I realized I wouldn't have to worry about offending anybody in the crowd. The DJ's songlist was brief—just a few pages, no longer than a subway-shop menu—and consisted mostly of standards, including some pop tunes from the '80s. Jenny and I spent a good ten minutes flipping through the song titles before eventually choosing Wham!'s "Wake Me Up before You Go-Go," as it seemed a bit less creepy than George Michael's "I Want Your Sex." Afterward, Mike and our friend Tom performed "Bennie and the Jets," a song that feels especially long when it's shrieked into a pair of low-range microphones. I looked at the waiting list and saw that the karaoke machine had been completely booked, and for the next half hour, I watched as bridesmaids, family friends, and even my new in-laws took turns at the front of the dance floor, maneuvering around the tiny karaoke stand. Just when the DJ was about to turn off the machine, I realized that one song was still missing.

"Do you think you could play 'New York, New York'?" I asked him.

My mom had told me for years that there was no way I'd ever get my father to sing at karaoke again, but I figured this would be my one opportunity to see what I'd missed in Hawaii. When the song started, Jenny and I took the microphones, and everybody was called to the floor. Many of the guests—perhaps wisely—opted to stay in their seats, but within a few seconds I could feel a crowd forming behind us, one that grew larger with each verse. I turned around and saw that even my father was a few feet away from me. I heard his singing voice for the first time in years and realized how much it sounded like my own.

At one point, I got carried away and separated myself from the group, knocked out of orbit on the dance floor. I felt a hand on my shoulder, and it was Jenny, pulling me back. Behind her was a circle of people, a backing group of every person I know and love.

I took her hand and went inside. There was no reason for me to keep singing by myself.

APPENDIX A: FIFTY SONGS I'LL NEVER STOP SINGING AT KARAOKE

1. "Sister Christian," Night Ranger
2. "Flagpole Sitta," Harvey Danger
3. "On Our Own," Bobby Brown
4. "Cold as Ice," Foreigner
5. "Brandy (You're a Fine Girl)," Looking Glass
6. "Raspberry Beret," Prince
7. "Buffalo Stance," Neneh Cherry
8. "Downtown," Petula Clark
9. "Wanted Dead or Alive," Bon Jovi
10. "No Scrubs," TLC
11. "I Want It That Way," Backstreet Boys
12. "Immigrant Song," Led Zeppelin
13. "Stand Back," Stevie Nicks
14. "Say Say Say," Paul McCartney and Michael Jackson
15. "Freedom '90," George Michael
16. "Steppin' Out," Joe Jackson

17. "Hate to Say I Told You So," The Hives
18. "Bennie & the Jets," Elton John
19. "We Built This City," Starship
20. "Godzilla," Blue Oyster Cult
21. "Regulate," Warren G feat. Nate Dogg
22. "I'm a Flirt," R. Kelly
23. "Dreams," Fleetwood Mac
24. "Love Is a Battlefield," Pat Benatar
25. "Massachusetts," Bee Gees
26. "Bringin' On the Heartbreak," Def Leppard
27. "One More Time," Daft Punk
28. "Disco 2000," Pulp
29. "Because of You," Ne-Yo
30. "Heartbreaker," Rolling Stones
31. "Pleasant Valley Sunday," Monkees
32. "Dream Police," Cheap Trick
33. "Rosanna," Toto
34. "Stop Draggin' My Heart Around," Tom Petty and Stevie Nicks
35. "Unforgettable Fire," U2
36. "Eleanor Put Your Boots On," Franz Ferdinand
37. "Get What You Give," New Radicals
38. "Sugar, We're Goin' Down," Fall Out Boy
39. "Come Dancing," The Kinks
40. "West End Girls," Pet Shop Boys
41. "Friday Night," The Darkness
42. "Love Plus One," Haircut 100
43. "That's All," Genesis
44. "Let's Wait Awhile," Janet Jackson
45. "Summer Breeze," Seals & Crofts

46. "Walk Away," Kelly Clarkson
47. "Holding Back the Years," Simply Red
48. "Linda Linda," The Blue Hearts
49. "Do They Know It's Christmas," Band Aid
50. "Bette Davis Eyes," Kim Carnes

APPENDIX B: THIRTY SONGS I'LL NEVER FIND AT KARAOKE

1. "I Could Never Take the Place of Your Man," Prince
2. "Less Than Zero (You and Me)," Glenn Danzig
3. "The Secret of My Success," Night Ranger
4. "Illegal Alien," Genesis
5. "In the City," Joe Walsh
6. "Too Young," Phoenix
7. "So It Goes," Nick Lowe
8. "Don't Disturb This Groove," The System
9. "Debra," Beck
10. "Skip Steps 1 & 3," Superchunk
11. "I Never Thought It Would Happen," The Rubinoos
12. "Where Have All the Rude Boys Gone," Ted Leo + the Pharmacists
13. "Zombie Zoo," Tom Petty
14. "The Visitors," ABBA
15. "I Want to See the Bright Lights Tonight," Richard & Linda Thompson
16. "Finest Worksong," R.E.M.
17. "Wearing & Tearing," Led Zeppelin

18. "Made in Japan," Buck Owens
19. "Surprise! You're Dead!," Faith No More
20. "Welcome to the Terrordome," Public Enemy
21. "Can You Get to That," Funkadelic
22. "We Don't Need This Fascist Groove Thing," Heaven 17
23. "Another Girl, Another Planet," The Only Ones
24. "Can't Hardly Wait," The Replacements
25. "The Good Life," Weezer
26. "Oh!" Sleater-Kinney
27. "I Wanna Destroy You," Soft Boys
28. "Pumping on Your Stereo," Supergrass
29. "Memories Can't Wait," Talking Heads
30. "Get Over You," The Undertones

NOTE ON SOURCES

Unless otherwise noted, all quotations in the book were taken directly from interviews that I conducted between January 2007 and June 2008 (usually in person or on the phone, and sometimes via e-mail). In Japan, I hired Robert Scott Field to interpret my interview with Daisuke Inoue, and a few months later, Field conducted three separate interviews with Kay Takagi, using questions I provided.

The following sources offered valuable background information, leads, and context:

Agay, Denes. *Best-Loved Songs of the American People.* Garden City, N.Y.: GuildAmerica Books, 1975.

"Akihiko 'Roger' Kurobe: Management Interview." *Transpacific* 9 (1994).

"Band's Firing Rocks Hot Club." *New York Post,* 14 Nov. 2004.

Bombeck, Erma. "Parents Plot Sweet Revenge with a Karaoke Player." *Dallas Morning News,* 5 Dec. 1994.

Cavanagh, Dr. Joyce. *Youth and Money.* University of Missouri, 2000, extension.missouri.edu/hes/youthmoney.ppt.

Cress, Doug. "Oh Say, Can You Sing." *Atlanta Journal-Constitution,* 16 April 1993.

Hershenson, Roberta. "Where Frustrated Singers Act Out Their Dreams." *New York Times,* 6 Oct. 1991.

Hirose, Toru. "Karaoke King Pioneer to Face Rivals Online." *Nikkei Weekly* (Japan), 12 Dec. 1994.

Hodges, Sam. "The Karaoke King: Perky Orlando Entrepreneur Dave Bellagamba Reigns over a Growing Empire." *Orlando Sentinel,* 6 May 1992.

Iyer, Pico. "Daisuke Inoue." *Time Asia,* 23 Aug. 1999.

"Japanese Custom Has Execs Singing a Different Tune." *Chicago Tribune,* 18 Dec. 1988.

Leeds, Jeff. "Karaoke CD Label Sues Rivals over Issue of Licensing." *New York Times,* 13 May 2005.

Max Fleischer's Ko-Ko Song Car-Tunes. Directed by Ray Pointer. DVD. Inkwell Images, 2002.

McNeill, David. "The Man Who Taught the World to Sing." *The Independent* (U.K.), 24 May 2006.

Micallef, Ken. "The Most Popular Band in America!" *Blender,* June-July 2001.

Moore, Jerry. "Ultimate Sing-Along." *Chicago Tribune,* 24 Jan. 1993.

Olenick, Doug. "Makers See Karaoke Soaring High." *HFD: The Weekly Home Furnishings Newspaper,* 1 Nov. 1993.

Pascual, Aixa M. "Striking the Right Chord." *BusinessWeek,* 10 June 2002.

Paumgarten, Nick. "Aunt Janny." *The New Yorker,* 1 Oct. 2007.

Punk Rock/Heavy Metal Karaoke: The Movie. Directed by Sonny Aronson. DVD. Creative Arson, 2001.

Reynolds, Amy L. "Audience Is the Star Attraction on Karaoke Night." *Orlando Sentinel,* 21 July 1991.

Ross, Michael E. "Giving Voice to Fantasies of Singing, in Public Yet." *New York Times,* 28 April 1989.

Schrage, Michael. "Karaoke Battles a Case of Laryngitis." *Los Angeles Times,* 25 March 1993.

"The Singing Machine Company, Inc.—Company History." FundingUniverse. http://www.fundinguniverse.com/company -histories/The-Singing-Machine-Company-Inc-Company -History.html.

Teen Market Profile. Magazine Publishers of America. 2004. http://www.magazine.org/content/files/teenprofile04.pdf.

Young, Josh. "They're All That." *Entertainment Weekly,* 12 March 1999.

Zhou, Xun, and Francesca Tarocco. *Karaoke: The Global Phenomenon.* London: Reaktion Books, 2007.

ACKNOWLEDGMENTS

This book would not have been possible were it not for the many karaoke fans, experts, and industry veterans who graciously allowed me to ask ridiculous questions. I only wish I'd been able to include all of their responses: Neil Altnew, Jon Anzalone, Marion Arakaki, Fred Arnold, Cindy Ball, Jennifer Banko, Paris Barclay, Bud Barnes, David Bellagamba, Mindy Birnbaum, Rick Blackwell, Kristen Carney, Mattias Cederlund, Robert Charles, Bob Clifford, Owen Comaskey, Vanessa Cooney, Julia Darling, Frank Deserto, Karl Detken, Monica DeTonnancourt, Abbey Dvorak, Royale Edward, Devin Emke, Sal Ferraro, Robert Scott Field, Tina Fischer, Abby Gennet, Jim Gerik, Diana Gonzales, Michael Moses Griffin, Vincent Guagenti, Atte Hujanen, Kari Hujanen, Vic Hundahl, Daisuke Inoue, Aaron Jaffe, Paul Jensen, Filip Kamieniarz, Bucky Kaopuiki, Juha Karvonen, Kelly Keagy, Rob Kemp, Barry Klazura, Irv Kratka, Roger Kurobe, Pierre Lawestig, Gabriella Lukacs, Allen Ma, K'Nesha Maddox, Donnie Marshall, Heidi Mattila, Marcello Maturana, John McDonough, Corina Susanna Mitchell, Lenny Morheim, John Nance, David Naughton, John Nipe, Norry Niven, Wendell Payne, Ed Pearson, Breukellen Riesgo, David Richman, Barbie Robbins, George Robbins, Michelle Robbins, Richard Sakoda, Colin Schiller, Courtney Schneider, Marvy del Rosario

Schuman, Derek Slep, Kurt Slep, Wade Starnes, Edward Steele, Lael Sturm, Kay Takagi, Ernie Taylor, Rico Vanian, Joey Walker, Julie Walter-Sgro, Tim Wipperman, Paulie Z, Donald Zuckerman, and Bowie Zunino.

I'm also extremely grateful to the friends and colleagues who aided me throughout the writing process, whether by offering feedback and advice, indulging in my long rants about karaoke, or letting me crash on their couch after a long night of research: Sonny Aronson, Andrew Beaujon, Adele Berne, Doug Brod, Scott Brown, Katy Caldwell, Robert Capps, Jim Cooke, Laura Davis, Bridget DeClerk, Jon Dolan, Dan Dratch, Tom Eaton, Michael Endelman, Michael Ewing, Elizabeth Fagan, Gillian Flynn, Chloe Weiss Galkin, Matthew Galkin, Caryn Ganz, Lacy Garrison, Ben Gruber, Dave Hamilton, Brandon Hayes, Sean Howe, A. J. Jacobs, Maura Johnston, Steve Kandell, Greg Kirschling, Chuck Klosterman, Chris Knutsen, Melissa Maerz, Craig Marks, Sia Michel, Nancy Miller, Mike Minervini, Koji Mizutani, Brett Nolan, Alison Owings, David Penick, Jonathan Perdue, Candice Rainey, Phoebe Reilly, Kevin Roddy, Chris Ryan, Evan Serpick, Katie Sigelman, Laura Sinagra, Dan Snierson, Andrew Sparks, Ken Tucker, Karen Valby, Patrick Voigt, Ryan Walker, Anja Weber, Jane White, and Josh Wolk. I also owe a great debt to those who helped me in the earliest stages of my writing career, including Annabel Bentley, Jamie Bufalino, Maggie Murphy, Michele Romero, Mary Kaye Schilling, and the late Anderson Jones.

Two contributions of special note: Steve Kurutz's advice helped me from going completely coconuts on numerous occasions. And Mike Kuhle's friendship served as a constant source of ideas and inspiration. Without Mike, many of the events in this book never would have occurred in the first place, and I look forward to sharing many more karaoke adventures with him in the coming years.

The members of my family—Bill, Kay, and Chris Raftery—offered unconditional support and love, as always. And I was moved by the generosity demonstrated by my extended family: Claudia and Allen Clark, Jeff Williams, Rich Williams, and Craig, Judy, and Lindsay Whipple.

My thanks to my agent, Jud Laghi, for encouraging me to pursue this idea, and to my editor, Ben Schafer, for helping me put everything together (and for letting me get away with multiple Bobby Brown jokes). I'm also grateful for the assistance of Renee Caputo and Kathy Streckfus, who kept a close watch on the book as it went through the editing process.

In the end, though, none of this would have happened without my wife, Jenny, who's surely the most loving and inexplicably patient woman in the world. She's forever my partner, in life and in song.

ABOUT THE AUTHOR

Brian Raftery grew up in Devon, Pennsylvania, and graduated from Penn State University. His features and essays have appeared in such publications as *Wired, GQ, Spin, Esquire,* and *Entertainment Weekly.* He lives in Brooklyn with his wife, Jenny, and can be reached at brianraftery@gmail.com.